# Reconciling Memories

. *Edited by* Alan D Falconer

# *Reconciling Memories*

the columba press

## the columba press

93 The Rise, Mount Merrion, Blackrock, Co. Dublin, Ireland

First edition 1988
Cover by Bill Bolger
Origination by Typeform Ltd, Dublin
Printed in Ireland by Genprint Ltd, Dublin

ISBN 0 948183 56 X

# Contents

# Acknowledgements

Without the encouragement, support and work of a large number of people this project would not have been brought to fruition. Thanks are due to the late Professor T.W. Moody for stimulating the ideas which eventually led to this volume; to the Executive Board of the Irish School of Ecumenics and its Director, the Rev. Dr. R.H.S. Boyd, for supporting the explorations of these ideas; to the Dutch-Northern Ireland Committee for sponsoring a seminar for a small group of participants on the work of René Girard; to the Politics and Forgiveness Project associated with the British Council of Churches and its Director, Mr. Brian Frost, for the invitation to participate in their Oxford theological conference, and thus learn from the experience and insights of others wrestling with similar questions; to the Centre for Theology and Public Issues of Edinburgh University and its Director, Rev. Principal Duncan Forrester and to the then Dean of King's College, London, the Rt. Rev. Richard Harries, who both welcomed the opportunity to sponsor conferences where the basic ideas of this project were further developed; and to the Netherlands Reformed Church and to the Inter Church Emergency Fund for Ireland, who have generously supported this project financially and have made possible this publication.

An immense debt of gratitude is due to the authors of the various papers who so willingly agreed to take part in the exploration of an idea; to my secretary, Miss Euphan Stephenson who has borne the brunt of the organization of successive seminars and has made intelligible the manuscripts in successive versions for this volume; to Sr. Helen Butterworth I.B.V.M. who has painstakingly compiled the Index for this volume; and to Mr. Sean O Boyle of Columba Press, Dublin, for his advice, encouragement and willingness to publish these papers.

Above all, I wish to thank my wife, Marjorie. Without her support the strength to undertake this voyage of discovery would have been lacking. Our children also, David, Rosalind and Andrew, have had repeated occasion to exercise the reconciling power of forgiveness on their distracted father.

i

*To the Memory*
*of*
*Theodore W. Moody*
*Professor of History and Fellow of the*
*University of Dublin, Trinity College*
*Member of the Academic Council*
*and Executive Board of the*
*Irish School of Ecumenics*
*(1971 — 1984)*

*whose life was dedicated to the work of*
*reconciling memories in Ireland*

# Preface

In his Nobel Lecture in 1980, Czeslaw Milosz observed that 'the new obsession is the refusal to remember'. During my first year as a teacher in the Irish School of Ecumenics, an incident occurred which would seem to run counter to that suggestion.

At that time, one of the courses of lectures given to the students concerned 'the Irish situation', in which an analysis of the history, politics, socio-economic and religious dimensions of Irish societies was undertaken by an English sociologist. Invariably, the Irish born students found this course problematic. One such student eventually became so angry that he articulated his frustrations and as a final seal to his statement produced from his wallet a certificate. 'This certificate' he said, 'was given to my family at the time of the famine. It is a certificate of disjunction from their land. I carry it in my wallet with me all the time.'

That memory had imprisoned the student. Undoubtedly the Famine was a tale of human disaster on an immense scale. Unquestionably, the Famine had political repercussions in Ireland. Yet that event of one and a quarter centuries ago seemed to determine the way that Irish student acted today. He was not in a position to enter any positive relations with people from England.

To a Scotsman, there' seemed to be an inability to interpret history. During the same period as the Famine, after all, an equally incredible tale of human misery and exploitation had occurred. Whole families and clans were removed from their lands in Scotland, in what has been called 'The Highland Clearances', so that sheep could be reared. Sheep were a more economically sound investment in the Highlands than people, so the people were shipped to Canada or the United States or they made their way to the Lowlands of Scotland seeking shelter and work. The Highland Clearances were no less inhuman in their effect than the Famine in Ireland, yet memory of the clearances does not seem to have the same imprisoning effect. For many in Ireland, as Oliver McDonagh notes in his *States of Mind,* the past is contemporary. A first impression then, might be that the observation of Milosz that 'the new obsession is the refusal to remember' would not be true in Ireland.

In years subsequent to that incident, opportunity to explore the question of the understanding of history informally with Professor Theo Moody presented itself on many occasions. From these conversations emerged the idea of exploring this further in a series of consultations. During this period the Field Day group were exploring the way in which the identity of the Anglo-Irish, Ulster Scot and Catholic Nationalist traditions in Ireland could be described and re-interpreted. Yet various questions still required exploration. How does a member of any of these traditions appropriate the history, literature and memories of that tradition, and have these traditions given any space to the fact that they had been responsible for the identity of the other traditions also? The history of the different traditions on these islands was and is interdependent. A third question might be the fact that each tradition was identified with a particular expression of Christianity, yet the Churches seemed to be unable to break through the captivity of the memories of the different traditions, despite the fact that 'to remember' in the Bible is to participate in a liberating event.

These questions set the agenda for the various papers in this volume. The contributions were presented at different consultations held in Dublin in April 1986 and Edinburgh and London in March 1987. In the light of comments made in discussion at the various Consultations some of the contributions have undergone development. The complexity of recording those discussions, however, since different papers were presented on different occasions, other than those of Frank Wright and myself which were delivered on the three occasions, has made it impossible to offer a digest of the proceedings. The papers are therefore offered as a contribution to the exploration of an idea. It is not that in Ireland 'the new obsession is the refusal to remember' as Czeslaw Milosz observed, but that the pervasive memories need to be reconciled, so that the different communities might be liberated.

*Alan D. Falconer*
*Reformation Day*
*31st October 1987*

# Introduction

## Alan D. Falconer

In his *The Book of Laughter and Forgetting*, the Czechoslovakian novelist Milan Kundera offers a series of reflections on the importance of memory as the root from which the self-understanding of their identities by individuals and groups emerges. In one of the essays in the book, he analyses the writing of Franz Kafka and comments:

> Prague in his novels is a city without memory. It has even forgotten its name. Nobody there remembers anything, nobody recalls anything . . . No song is capable of uniting the city's present with its past by recalling the moment of its birth.

> Time in Kafka's novel is the time of a humanity that has lost its continuity with humanity, of a humanity that no longer knows anything nor remembers anything, that lives in nameless cities with nameless streets or streets different from the ones they had yesterday, because a name means continuity with the past and people without a past are people without a name.[1]

In his essays Kundera explores this theme in relation to the way in which an attempt has been made by the State authorities to change the awareness of the identity of the Czech people since the end of the Second World War. An attempt has been made to erase the nation's memory, and through this the identity of the people has been eroded. As Kundera notes when he quotes his friend Milan Hubl approvingly:

> The first step in liquidating a people is to erase its memory.[2]

The culture, traditions, songs, religious commitment, political ideals embodied above all in the literature and poetry of the community are important vehicles communicating and challenging the identity of the society. The awareness of the history of the community highlights the struggles, ideals and mistakes made by and in relation to the community. The cohesiveness and sense of direction of the community is nourished by its memories.

The importance of 'memories' for the nourishing of 'identity' is particularly evident in Ireland. Events in the seventeenth and early twentieth centuries are celebrated in song, poem, 'history lessons' and the gathering of the community.[3] The hurt, dislocation, and deaths of the famine and clearances condition peoples' response to others, and are the subject of a considerable literature.[4] The achievements and the struggles of individuals and groups, the sense of awakening and the oppressive weight of despair, evident in the literature, songs and postures of communities in Ireland, have shaped the very identity of the communities in Ireland.

These memories, however, can not only shape the identities of the various communities, but also imprison the communities. John Hewitt in 'Postscript 1984' writes:

The years deceived: our unforgiving hearts,
by myths and old antipathies betrayed,
flared into sudden acts of violence
in daily shocking bulletins relayed,
and through our dark dream-clotted consciousness
hosted like banners in some bleak parade.

Now with compulsive resonance they toll;
Banbridge, Ballykelly, Darkley, Crossmaglen,
summoning pity, anger and despair,
by grief of kin, by hate of murderous men
till the whole tarnished map is stained and torn,
not to be read as pastoral again.[5]

John Hewitt well conveys the cyclical sense of history so evident in the memory of the different traditions in Ireland.

Among the Protestant community there is a 'siege mentality'. Protestants tend to remember those occasions in their history when they have been under siege from Roman Catholic forces. Thus the history lessons emphasise 1641 when the Earls rose against the Protestants to try to reclaim the land given to the incomers; and subsequent dates highlight those occasions when a similar situation arose and when a state of siege ensued. The siege mentality arises from the sense of the repetitiveness of history. It informs the rhetoric and the politics of Northern Ireland. This memory imprisons the community, and makes it difficult to pursue a more open attitude to other communities. As Hewitt puts it:

Now with compulsive resonance they toll;
Banbridge, Ballykelly, Darkley, Crossmaglen,
summoning pity, anger and despair

– contemporary instances which seem to repeat an old story.

While there exists a 'siege mentality' among Protestants in Northern Ireland, there is a 'coercion mentality' among Roman Catholics – a sense of being colonized and of having freedom limited by another community. Within this coercion mentality is a memory that independence and freedom has had to be asserted through force of arms. The Proclamation of the Republic on Easter Monday 1916 refers to six previous occasions when this pattern of history had occurred – 1916

2

being the seventh such occasion. I am not stressing here that the Roman Catholic community affirms violence – that would be too facile, and would not carry the constant denunciations of violence as part of the story. In using this example I simply want to stress that here also is evident a cyclical attitude to history – a sense that the same forces are at work constantly in the story, and thus the memory of this community.[6] Once again, history holds a community captive. The awareness of the cyclical nature of history is seen to match the intricate patterns of Irish Celtic art. The memory imprisons.

In recent years, attempts have been made to explore the identities of each community in Ireland through an examination of its appropriation of history and the articulation of its identity in literature, gesture, kinship and myth, to break through the captivity of memories. The *Field Day* pamphlets and *The Crane Bag* have been a stimulating expression of this contemporary exploration.[7] In relation to the identities of the Anglo-Irish, Ulster Scot and Irish Nationalist traditions the pamphlets have stepped

. . . through origins
like a dog turning
its memories of wilderness
on the kitchen mat

as Seamus Heaney has put it.[8] The differing communities have been empowered to recover the memories of their origins and, by this exposure to the myths of their histories and to those events in their histories and literature which have not been to the foreground of their contemporary memories, to rephrase their identity.[9] Unlike Kafka's Prague, Ireland is a land of memories, of consciousness of those memories and of identities whose contours are moulded by these memories.

Ireland's characteristic is, therefore, not that it is a city without a name, but a land where everything has two or three names. The various traditions and communities, while they have explored their own memories in the search for their identity, have not always faced up to the interdependence of the communities.[10]

John Beckett in *The Anglo Irish Tradition* stresses that at times the identity of the community was shaped in opposition to the other communities in Ireland:

In the long run it is perhaps by their attitude to the Roman Catholics rather than by their attitude to England that the political outlook of the Anglo-Irish can be clearly assessed, though the two attitudes are sometimes closely interdependent.[11]

This identity-in-opposition was true not only for political attitudes. It is also evident in the theological stances of the communities. Thus theology was often conducted in a way which asserted the difference between one community and another in Ireland. As one example of this from the tradition of the Church of Ireland, one might cite T.C. Hammond's book *The One Hundred Texts* which highlights what is deemed to be the one hundred basic texts in the Bible by which the author proceeds briefly to show how Anglicans have understood these texts correctly, and then at great length shows how the Roman Catholic Church has misunderstood them. That such a theological method is not yet dead may be seen in the well written and eirenic booklet by Victor Griffin, Dean of St. Patrick's Catheral, Dublin, entitled *Anglican and Irish: What We Believe*. Despite its title the booklet is an attempt to overcome some of the traditional difficulties which Anglicans have had with some Roman Catholic theological positions. The impression might be received that Anglican Irish identity is an identity phrased in opposition to Roman Catholicism.

That this is not simply an Anglican tendency has been emphasised by Prof. Patrick Corish of St. Patrick's College, Maynooth, in his recent study of *The Irish Catholic Experience*. Prof. Corish notes that post-Reformation Roman Catholic theological education emphasised the importance of learning the theological treatises rather than the Bible. Through the appropriation of these treatises it was felt that Roman Catholic identity would be affirmed as an identity-in-opposition to Protestants. 'Now to be a Catholic, was not to be a Protestant.'[12]

This identity-in-opposition has led to an emphasis on the independence of each tradition in Ireland. Yet it is quite clear that such identity is interdependent. The independence, however, of each tradition has been continually proclaimed and maintained. The communities have found it difficult to listen to each other. The 'other' has not been part of our world view.

In a poem entitled 'The Legend' in his recent collection of poems, the Scots poet Iain Crichton Smith trenchantly observes:

The anthology of memories of the other
is a book I hadn't reckoned on . . .[13]

The identities and memories of the communities have co-existed — often uneasily — in Ireland, and at times have confronted each other. Yet has enough attention been paid to the interdependence of the traditions — to the fact that the actions, postures and identities of one community have shaped the identity of other communities? The time is more than ripe for the task of 'reconciliation of memories'.[14]

While there is great consciousness of 'memories' and their impact on the identity of communities in Ireland, there is also a lot of talk about the need for reconciliation in Ireland and for the reconciliation of identities. A variety of institutes and centres have been established to foster 'reconciliation'.[15] The word has entered our contemporary vocabulary to such an extent that the warning of Dietrich Bonhoeffer, the German theologian, seems apposite. In a course of lectures and seminars conducted in the University of Berlin fifty years ago, on the topic of discipleship, Bonhoeffer began by warning of the dangers of what he called 'cheap grace', or cheap reconciliation.

4

Cheap grace means grace sold on the market like cheap jack's wares. The sacraments, the forgiveness of sin, and the consolations of religion are thrown away at cut prices. Grace is represented as the Church's inexhaustible treasury, from which she showers blessings with generous hands, without asking questions or fixing limits. Grace without price; grace without cost! . . . Cheap grace means grace as a doctrine, a principle, a system. It means forgiveness of sins proclaimed as a general truth . . . An intellectual assent to that idea is held to be of itself sufficient.[16]

Reconciliation cannot be cheap and and failure to bear its cost will intensify alienation and the separation of our different memories and histories.

To explore the theme 'the reconciliation of memories', then, involves not only 'reckoning with the other's memories' as Iain Crichton Smith put it, but also examining the nature of 'reconciliation', and being prepared to bear the cost of such a costly reconciliation.

The cost of reconciliation was a constant theme in the writings of the Russian novelist, Leo Tolstoy, especially those works produced in the period 1886-1897. In *Father Sergius, The Kreutzer Sonata, The Devil,* and *What I Believe,* Tolstoy explores the breakdown of relationships and the need for reconciliation, and the way in which the behaviour of one person affects the identity of others. The costliness of reconciliation is nowhere more eloquently and perceptively exposed than in Tolstoy's novel *Resurrection,* written in this period. The plot, based on a real episode, told to Tolstoy by his friend Koni, tells of a nobleman who was called to serve on a jury at the trial of a prostitute for murder. The Prince recognized in her a girl whom in his youth he had seduced. The novel wrestles with the question of how the nobleman and the prostitute can be reconciled. In such a situation, it is evident that to ask forgiveness is not enough. The Prince finds it necessary to transform his life by taking responsibility for his actions through the appropriating of the prostitute's story. Initially, of course, his action is governed by his desire to be freed from his own sense of guilt. The prostitute, equally, is hesitant about accepting the seriousness of the Prince's desire for forgiveness until she sees the way he seeks to offer reparation by centring his life on her needs. Forgiveness emerges when each eventually is empowered to be free. Resurrection occurs. Out of the despair and alienation of fractured relationship, hope, new life and new creation are born through the acceptance of responsibility and the appropriation of the history of the other.

Memory need not imprison, therefore. Indeed, what Tolstoy in his writings has managed to recapture is the biblical concept of memory, where memory does not captivate, but liberates.

For the people of Israel, the injunction to remember which was especially evident in the Passover celebration and in the great autumn festival associated with the harvest, involved the re-appropriation of God's liberating activity when he brought the people out of Egypt. The Passover was an appropriating of the event of liberation recalling God's promise, his Word which was made effective by Him with regard to the people.

In the New Testament, above all in the Book of Hebrews, this activity of remembrance (*anamnesis*) is paralled with God's remission of sins. God is seen in Jesus Christ to have taken upon himself the history of humankind. God has appropriated our story. It is once again in worship that the injunction to remember is prominent. The celebration of the Lord's Supper is a celebration and a re-appropriation of God's activity in Jesus Christ liberating humankind so that human beings might be free to respond to God and to each other.[17] As the recent Faith and Order Report, *Baptism, Eucharist and Ministry* puts it:

> Christ himself with all that he has accomplished for us and for all creation (in his incarnation, servanthood, ministry, teaching, suffering, sacrifice, resurrection, ascension and sending of the Spirit) is present in this *anamnesis,* granting us communion with himself.[18]

Memory for the Scriptures is a liberating event in the context of God's activity in taking upon himself our history, forgiving us and freeing us to relate to himself and each other.

Such a concept of memory involves the acceptance of responsibility for the other. the appropriation of the history of the other. Such a reconciliation of memories, a reconciliation of histories, will involve, as Tolstoy has shown, the cleansing of memories.

In a recent address to the Swiss Protestant Federation, Pope John Paul II emphasised that

> cleansing our memories will include the frank recognition of mutual wrongs and errors in our behaviour towards one another.[19]

Such a recognition involves our acceptance of responsibility for the hurt in the memory of the other, and the attempt together to acknowledge our inter-relatedness.

Reconciliation cannot be 'cheap'. Reconciliation involves the recognition of the interdependence of our histories. Reconciliation entails the appropriation of each other's history, through which each empowers the other to be free. Through the reconciliation of memories a new identity is born.

The Scots poet Edwin Muir phrases this vision thus:

> Now in this iron reign
> I sing the liberty
> Where each asks from each
> What each most wants to give
> And each awakes in each
> What else would never be,
> Summoning so the rare
> Spirit to breathe and live.[20]

6

# NOTES

1. Milan Kundera *The Book of Laughter and Forgetting* trans. Michael H. Heim, Harmondsworth, Penguin 1983, p 157.
   See also my own article 'A Visit to the U.S.S.R.' in *Doctrine and Life* 34(10)85 pp 587-595, with particular reference to Lithuania.
2. ibid. p 159.
3. See for example Austin Clarke 'Celebrations' in Maurice Harmon (ed) *Irish Poetry after Yeats* Dublin, Wolfhound Press 1981, p 36f, and Séamus Deane *History Lessons* Dublin, Gallery Press 1983. This theme is evident in the writings and poems of many contemporary Irish writers from both parts of Ireland.
4. See for example Seán ÓTuama (ed) *An Duanaire* 1600-1900: Poems of the Dispossessed, trans. Thomas Kinsella, Portlaoise, Dolmen Press 1981.
5  John Hewitt *Freehold and Other Poems* Belfast, Blackstaff 1986, p 26f. See also Oliver McDonagh *States of Mind:* A Study of Anglo-Irish Conflict 1780-1980, London, George Allen & Unwin, 1983.
6. See Padraig O'Malley *The Uncivil Wars:* Ireland Today, Belfast, Blackstaff Press 1983.
7. The first six of the Field Day pamphlets have been published as *Ireland's Field Day* by Hutchinson (London) 1985. The authors included Tom Paulin, Séamus Heaney, Séamus Deane, Richard Kearney, Declan Kiberd and Denis Donoghue. A further three pamphlets by Terence Brown, Marianne Elliott and Robert McCartney were published in 1985.
   Many of the concerns of the Field Day authors are apparent also in the various issues of *The Crane Bag* edited by M. Patrick Hederman and Richard Kearney.
8. Séamus Heaney 'Kinship' in Maurice Harmon op.cit. p 212.
9. cf. the Presbyterian dissenting tradition and the co-operation between Presbyterians and Roman Catholics in the eightheenth and early nineteenth centuries which is a 'suppressed memory' of most Presbyterians today.
10. The plea for an exploration of the interdependence of the traditions is made by Terence McCaughey in his review of the *Field Day* pamphlets in *Fortnight* 9th September 1985, p 21.
11. John Beckett *The Anglo-Irish Tradition* Belfast, Blackstaff Press 1983, p 53.
12. T.C. Hammond *The One Hundred Texts* Dublin, Society for Irish Church Missions 1966, (orig. 1932). Victor Griffin *Anglican and Irish: What We Believe* Dublin, APCK 1976. Patrick Corish *The Irish Catholic Experience* Dublin, Gill & Macmillan 1985.
13. Iain Crichton Smith *The Exiles* Dublin, Raven Arts Press and Manchester, Coronet Press 1984, p 36.
14. The phrase 'The Reconciliation of Memories' which appeared as the title for our Consultation derives from a suggestive and thoughtful essay with that title by Mark Santer, Bishop of Kensington, and co-chairman of the Anglican-Roman Catholic International Commission, in M. Santer (ed) *Their Lord and Ours* London SPCK 1982.
15. See Ian Ellis (ed) *Peace and Reconciliation Projects in Ireland:* A Directory, Armagh 1983.
16. Dietrich Bonhoeffer *The Cost of Discipleship* London, SCM 1959, p 35.
17. See Max Thurian *Eucharistic Memorial* transl. J.G. Davies Ecumenical Studies in Worship no. 7, 2 vols. London, Lutterworth 1961.
18. Faith and Order *Baptism, Eucharist, Ministry* Faith and Order Paper no. 111, Geneva, WCC 1982, par. 6.
19. John Paul II, Address to the Swiss Protestant Church Federation 1984 cited in Bernard Sesboüé 'A Right and a Wrong Way to Celebrate' in *The Ecumenical Review* 39(1)87, p 89.
20. Edwin Muir 'The Annunciation' in his *Collected Poems* London, Faber 1960 p 117.

# Myth and the Critique of Tradition

*Richard Kearney*

There has been much talk in recent years about reconciling traditions in Ireland. But before traditions can be properly reconciled, it is first necessary to understand how and why traditions play such an important role in our contemporary lives. What is their origin, their *raison d'être*, their end? Why doesn't the past just go away and let us get on with the future? Is it not time that sons buried their fathers and started living their own lives in a free and creative manner? The recent debates in *Crane Bag* and the *Field Day* pamphlets have sought to address some of these questions. But in addition to analysing the specific *contents* of our Irish traditions – social, literary, religious and political – it is perhaps also necessary to offer a more philosophical account of the *form* of tradition in general. In this paper, I attempt to outline some aspects of such a philosophical account by looking at the central role played by myth in our understanding of tradition. Myth, I argue, is not some neutral museum piece of the ancient past; it is a living dimension of culture which may serve either a negative *ideological* or a positive *utopian* function. The argument I propose here is, in many respects, a theoretical development of my conclusion to the *Field Day* pamphlet *Myth and Motherland*, to the effect that every tradition needs to be both demythologized and remythologized. Without such an ongoing process of critical and creative reinterpretation, there is, I am convinced, little hope for any realistic reconciliation of the different cultural traditions on this island.

# 1

A major question arising from the contemporary conflict between tradition and modernity is that of the role of *myth*. The modernist break with the past usually took the form of a *demythologizing* project. While this project was a necessary corrective to the conservative apotheosis of tradition – the belief that the past constitutes some inviolable monolith of truth – it can also be pushed to extremes.

In the field of contemporary aesthetic theory, the 'textual revolution' has occasionally yielded excessive versions of formalism, subjectivism and even nihilism. The impulse to deconstruct tradition at all costs and in every context, has been known to result in anti-humanist celebrations of the 'disappearance of man'.[1] And in the process history itself, as the life-world of social interaction between human agents, is eclipsed. Being effectively reduced to a 'prison house of language' (i.e. to an endless intertextual play of signifiers), the very concept of history is drained of human content and social commitment. It is deprived of its memory. It falls casuality to the amnesia of the absolute text.

In the sphere of politics, the project of demythologization has sometimes led to a full-scale declaration of war against the past. Marx anticipated such a move in *The Eighteenth Brumaire* when he distinguished between the revolution which draws its inspiration from the past, 'calling up the dead upon the universal stage of history', and the revolution which creates itself 'out of the future', discarding the 'ancient superstitions' of tradition and letting the 'dead bury the dead in order to discover its own meaning'.[2] The danger of the demythologizing strategy occurs when it is pressed into the service of a self-perpetuating iconoclasm which, if left unchecked, liquidates the notion of the past altogether. Modern consciousness may thus find itself liberated into a no-mans-land of interminable self-reflection without purpose or direction. It is not enough to free a society *from* the 'false consciousness' of tradition, one must also liberate it *for* something. And this raises the question of 'memory' – and by extension 'myth' (understood in the broad sense of a collective symbolic project) – as a potentially positive and emancipatory force in its own right.

The attempt to erase historical remembrance can result in enslavement to the ephemeral immediacies of the present. It is a mistake to oppose in an absolute fashion the utopian impulses of modernity to the recollective impulses of tradition. For a culture invents its future by reinventing its past. And here we might usefully contrast Nietzsche's 'active forgetting' of history (which so readily degenerates into the 'ludic disportings of disruption and desire') with Benjamin's more subtle notion of 'revolutionary nostalgia' – an active remembering which reinterprets the suppressed voices of tradition in a critical rapport with modernity.[3] It is this latter model which the Frankfurt School, and in particular Marcuse, had in mind when they developed the dialectical notion of an 'anticipatory memory' (*vordeutende Erinnerung*) capable of projecting future images of liberation drawn from the past. The rediscovery of the subterranean history of the past as a 'presage of possible truth' can yield critical standards which are tabooed in the present. Recollecting the discarded aspirations of tradition thus triggers a liberating return of the repressed. The *recherche du temps perdu* becomes the vehicle of future emancipation.[4] Marcuse spells out some of the radical implications of this anticipatory memory as follows:

> Utopia in great art is never the simple negation of the reality principle (of history) but its transcending preservation in which past and present cast their shadow on fulfillment. The authentic utopia is grounded in recollection. 'All reification is forgetting' . . . Forgetting past suffering and past joy alleviates life under a repressive reality principle. In contrast, remembrance spurs the drive for the conquest of suffering and the permanence of joy . . . the horizon of history

9

is still open. If the remembrance of things past would become a motive power in the struggle for changing the world, the struggle would be waged for a revolution hitherto suppressed in the previous historical revolutions.[5]

# II

How does this relate to the dialectic of tradition and modernity which this paper has been exploring in the context of Irish culture?

In a recent commemorative address for Thomas Ashe (the 1916 patriot who died on hunger strike a year after the Easter rebellion), Sean MacBride, winner of the Nobel and Lenin peace prizes and a former Minister in the Irish government, accused 'many of our so-called intellectuals' of devaluing the 'concepts of Irish nationality and even the principles upon which Christianity is founded'. MacBride deplored the absence of idealism and the erosion of moral standards which were causing young people in Ireland today to despair and to be cynical. Our national pride, he observed, was being corroded by the emergence of an insidious double-talk and the resurgence of the slave mentality which existed prior to 1916. "It seems to me", MacBride concluded, "as if we are at a crossroads at which the choice has to be made between idealism and possibly sacrifice or betrayal and an abandonment of our national tradition and goals."[6]

MacBride is quite justified in reminding intellectuals of their obligation to respect the positive heritage of their tradition. He is also no doubt correct in warning against the fashionable tendency to summarily dismiss the very concepts of nationality, religion and cultural identity as so many outworn ideologies. (Indeed as even the Marxist critic Frederic Jameson remarked, 'a Left which cannot grasp the immense Utopian appeal of nationalism, any more than it can that of religion . . . must effectively doom itself to political impotence'.[7] MacBride is labouring under a severe misapprehension, however, if he rebukes all intellectual attempts to critically question or reinterpret tradition as perfidy and betrayal. Tradition can only be handed over (*tradere*) from one historical generation to the next by means of an ongoing process of innovative translation. And if tradition inevitably entails translation it equally entails transition. The idea that there exists some immutable 'essence' of national identity, timelessly preserved in the mausoleum of a sealed tradition and impervious to critical interrogation, is a nonsense. Tradition can only be transmitted through the indispensable detour of multiple translations, each one of which involves both critical discrimination and creative reinvention.

Gone are the days, fortunately, when intellectuals were expected to serve the nation by parroting simplistic formulae such as 'Up the Republic' and 'Keep the Faith' – or, north of the border, 'No Surrender' and 'Home Rule is Rome Rule'. Gone also, one would hope, are the days when Irish intellectuals could be branded by a government Minister as 'pinko liberals and Trinity queers', or have their works banned because they raised questions which were better not discussed (a sorry phenomenon which prompted one distinguished commentator to cite 'anti-intellectualism' among the seven pillars of Irish political culture)[8]. "Irish intellectuals have been accused of almost everything, from elitism to indifference and from subversion to being drunk and refusing to fight . . . Frequently these charges were trumped up because people in general, and their leaders in particular, did not take kindly to the idea of arguing with awkward customers about issues which, in the interests of peaceful existence, ought to be left alone. For the politicians and the Churches, such people were particularly troublesome . . . and the label 'intellectual' was tied to their names to show that they were at least boring and at worst dangerous."[9] Enough is enough.

The need to perpetually re-evaluate one's cultural heritage raises, once again, the central questions of *narrative*. Narrative – understood as the universal human desire to make sense of history by making a story – relates to tradition in two ways. By creatively reinterpreting the past, narrative can serve to release new and hitherto concealed possibilities of understanding one's history; and by critically scrutinizing the past it can wrest tradition away from the conformism that is always threatening to overpower it.[10] To properly attend to this dual capacity of narrative is, therefore, to resist the habit of establishing a dogmatic opposition between the 'eternal verities' of tradition, on the one hand, and the free inventiveness of critical imagination, on the other. Every narrative interpretation, as Alasdair MacIntyre reminds us, whether it involves a literary or political reading of history, "takes place within the context of some traditional mode of thought, transcending through criticism and invention the limitations of what had hitherto been reasoned in that tradition . . . Traditions when vital embody continuities of conflict".[11] This implies that the contemporary act of re-reading (i.e. re-telling) tradition can actually disclose uncompleted and disrupted narratives which open up unprecedented possibilities of understanding. No text exists in a vacuum, in splendid isolation from its social and historical contexts. And tradition itself is not some seamless monument existing beyond time and space – as the revivalist orthodoxy would have us believe – but a narrative construct requiring an open-ended process of reinterpretation. To examine one's culture, consequently, is also to examine one's conscience – in the sense of critically discriminating between rival interpretations. And this is a far cry from the agonising inquest conducted by revivalists into the supposedly 'unique essence' of national identity. Séamus Deane is right, I believe, when he pleads for the abandonment of the idea of essence – 'that hungry Hegelian ghost looking for a stereotype to live in' – since our national heritage, be it literary or political, is something which has always to be rewritten. Only such a realisation can enable a new writing and a new politics, 'unblemished by Irishness, but securely Irish'.[12]

# III

I will now examine the more specific hermeneutic context of the demythologizing project which so powerfully informs modern thinking. Most contemporary critics of myth have focussed on its ideological role as a mystifying consciousness. Their critical approach has been termed a 'hermeneutics of suspicion' in that it negatively interprets (gr. *hermeneuein*) myth as a masked discourse which conceals a *real* meaning behind an *imaginary* one. [13]

The modern project of unmasking myth frequently takes its cue from the investigative methods developed by Marx, Nietzsche and Freud – the 'three masters of suspicion' as Ricoeur calls them. Nietsche advanced a genealogical hermeneutic which aimed to trace myths back to an underlying will to power (or in the case of the Platonic and Christian myths of otherworldly transcendence, to a negation of this will to power). Freud developed a psychoanalytic hermeneutic which saw myths as ways of disguising unconscious desires. Thus in *Totem and Taboo*, for example, Freud identifies myth as a substitution for lost primitive or infantile objects which provide symbolic compensation for prohibited pleasures. As such, religious myths are said to represent a sort of collective 'obsessional neurosis' whereby libidinal drives are repressed and concealed through a highly sophisticated mechanism of inhibition and sublimation. And thirdly, there is Marx who proposed a critical hermeneutic of 'false consciousness' aimed at exposing the hidden connection between ideological myths (or superstructures) and the underlying realities of class domination exemplified in the struggle for the ownership of the means of production (or infrastructures). Thus for Marx, the myth of a transcendental timeless fulfilment – whether it is projected by religion, art or philosophy – is in fact an ideological masking of the historical reality of socio-economic exploitation.

Marx shares with Nietzsche and Freud the suspicion that myth conceals itself as an imaginary project of false values. It is 'myth' precisely in the sense of illusion or deception for it inverts the true priority of the real over the imaginary, of the historical over the eternal. Hence the need for a negative hermeneutics of unmasking. The critique of myth is, accordingly, 'the categorical refusal of all relations where man finds himself degraded, imprisoned or abandoned'.[14] And in this respect, Marx's denunciation of the mythico-religious character of the great money fetish in the first book of *Capital* constitutes one of the central planks of his critique of ideology. Moreover, it is this equation of myth with the fetishization of false consciousness which animates Roland Barthes' famous structuralist critique of bourgeois 'mythologies' (where he argues that myth is an ideological strategy for reducing the social processes of History to timeless commodities of Nature).[15]

The negative hermeneutics of myth was by no means confined to the atheistic masters of suspicion. Many religious thinkers in the twentieth century have also endorsed the demythologising project. Indeed the very term 'demythologisation' is frequently associated with · the theological writings of Rudolph Bultmann. Bultmann held that Christianity must be emancipated from those 'mythic' accretions whereby Christ became idolized as the sacrificial Kyrios of a saviour cult . . . modelled on the pagan heroes of Hellenic or Gnostic mystery-rites.[16] Bultmann's demythologizing is levelled against the mystification of authentic Christian spirituality. His critique casts a suspecting glance at all efforts to reduce the genuine scandal of the Cross and Resurrection to an ideological system wherein the newness of the Christian message is ignored or betrayed. Bultmann systematically exposes the manner in which the Living Word of the Gospels often degenerated into cultic myths – e.g. the attempt to express the eschatological promise of the Kingdom as a cosmological myth of heaven and hell; or the attempt to reduce the historical working of the Spirit through the Church to a myth of triumphalistic power. To 'demythologize' Christianity is, for Bultmann, to dissolve these false scandals so as to let the true scandal of the Word made flesh speak to us anew.

In recent years this work of theistic demythologization has been effectively developed by the French thinker René Girard. Girard holds that the most radical aim of the Judaeo-Christian Revelation is to expose and overcome the mythic foundation of pagan religions in the ritual sacrifice of an innocent scapegoat. Imaginatively projecting the case of all disharmony and evil on to some innocent victim, a society contrives to hide from itself the real cause of its *internal* crisis. True Christianity rejects the cultic mythologizing of the scapegoat, deployed by societies as an ideological means of securing consensus. Only by demythologizing this ideological lie of sacrificial victimage, that is, by revealing the true innocence of the scapegoat Christ, can Christianity serve as a genuinely anti-mythic and anti-sacrificial religion.[17]

# IV

What all these exponents of the hermeneutics of suspicion – theist or atheist – have in common is a determination to debunk the ideological masking of a true meaning behind a mythologized meaning. While confirming the necessity for such a demythologizing strategy, we must ask if this critique is not itself subject to critique. In this way, we may be able to recognize another more liberating dimension of myth – the genuinely *utopian* – behind its negative *ideological* dimension. Only by supplementing the hermeneutics of suspicion with what Ricoeur calls a hermeneutics of affirmation, do we begin to discern the potentiality of myth for a positive symbolizing project which surpasses its falsifying content.[18]

But before proceeding to a discussion of the utopian horizon of myth we briefly rehearse the main ideological functions of myth – *integration, dissimulation* and *domination*. For it is only by smashing the ideological idols of myth that we can begin to let its utopian symbols speak. No contemporary consideration of myth can dispense with the critique of ideology. All remythologization presupposes demythologization. In an essay entitled 'Science and ideology' Ricoeur isolates three major traits of ideology:

1. *Myth as Integration*. Ideology expresses a social group's need for a communal set of images whereby it can represent itself to itself and to others. Most societies invoke a tradition of mythic idealizations whereby they may be aligned with a stable, predictable and repeatable order of meanings. This process of ideological self-representation frequently assumes the form of a mythic reiteration of the founding-act of the community. It seeks to redeem society from the contingencies or crises of the present by justifying its actions in terms of some sanctified past, some sacred Beginning.[19] One might cite here the role played by the Aeneas myth in Roman society or the cosmogony myths in Greek society or indeed the Celtic myths of Cuchulain and the Fianna in Irish society. And where an ancient past is lacking, a more recent past will suffice: e.g. the Declaration of Independence for the USA, the October Revolution for the USSR and so on.

Ideology thus serves to relate the social memory of an historical community to some inaugural act which founded it and which can be repeated over time in order to preserve a sense of social integration. Ricoeur defines the role of ideology thus:

not only to diffuse the conviction beyond the circle of founding fathers, so as to make it the creed of the entire group; its role is also to perpetuate the initial energy beyond the period of effervescence. It is into this gap, characteristic of all situations après coup, that the images and interpretations intervene. A founding act can be revived and reactualised only . . . through a representation of itself. The ideological phenomenon thus begins very early: for domestication by memory is accompanied not only by consensus, but also by convention and rationalisation (in the Freudian sense). At this point, ideology . . . continues to be mobilising only insofar as it is justificatory.[20]

The ideological recollection of sacred foundational acts has the purpose therefore of both integrating and justifying a social order. While this can accompany a cultural or national revival, it can also give rise to what Ricoeur calls a 'stagnation of politics' where 'each power initiates and repeats an anterior power: every prince wants to be Caesar, every Caesar wants to be Alexander, every Alexander wants to hellenise an Oriental despot'.[21] Either way, ideology entails a process of codification, schematization and ritualization, a process which stereotypes social action and permits a social group to recollect itself in terms of rhetorical maxims and idealized self-images.

2. *Myth as Dissimulation*. If the schematic 'rationalisations' of ideology bring

14

about social integration, they do so, paradoxically, at a 'pre-rational' or pre-conscious level. The ideology of foundational myths operates behind our backs, as it were, rather than appearing as a transparent theme before our eyes. We think *from* ideology rather than *about* it. And it is precisely because the codes of ideology function in this indirect and oblique manner that the practice of distortion and dissimulation can occur. This is the epistemological reason for Marx denouncing ideology as the falsifying projection of 'an inverted image of our own position in society'.[22] Ideology is by its very nature an 'uncritical instance' and thus easily susceptible to deceit, alienation – and by extension, intolerance. All too frequently, ideology functions in a reactionary or at least socially conservative fashion. 'It signifies that what is new can be accommodated only in terms of the typical, itself stemming from the sedimentation of social experience.'[23] Consequently, the future – as opening up that which is unassimilable and unprecedented vis-à-vis the pre-existing codes of experience – is often translated back into the orthodox stereotypes of the past. This accounts for the fact that many social groups display traits of ideological orthodoxy which render them intolerant towards what is marginal, different or alien. Pluralism and permissiveness are the bêtes noires of such social orthodoxy. They represent the intolerable. This phenomenon of ideological intolerance arises when the experience of radical novelty threatens the possibility of the social group recognizing itself in a retrospective reference to its hallowed traditions and orthodox pieties.

But ideology can also function in a dissimulating capacity to the extent that it conceals the gap between what *is* and what *ought* to be, that is, between our presently lived *reality* and the *ideal* world of our traditional self-representations.[24] By masking the gulf which separates our contemporary historical experience from our mythic memory, ideology often justifies the status quo by presuming that nothing has really changed. This self-dissimulation expresses itself as a resistance to change, as a closure to new possibilities of self-understanding. Whence the danger of reducing the challenge of the new to acceptable limits of an already established heritage of meaning.

*3. Myth as Domination.* This property of ideology raises the vexed question of the hierarchical organization of society – the question of authority. As Max Weber and later Jürgen Habermas observed, social systems tend to *legitimate* themselves by means of an ideology which justifies their right to secure and retain power.[25] This process of legitimation is inherently problematic, however, in so far as there exists a disparity between the nation/state's ideological *claim* to authority and the answering *belief* of the public. Ideology thus entails a surplus-value of claim over response, of power over freedom, (or as Sartre would put it, of essence over existence). Put another way, if a system's claim to authority were fully and

15

reciprocally consented to by those whom it governs there would be no urgent need for the persuasive or coercive strategies of ideological myths. Ideology operates accordingly as a 'surplus-value' symptomatic of the assymetry between the legitimizing 'ought' of our normative traditions, on the one hand, and the 'is' of our lived social existence, on the other. It is because there is no transparent or total coincidence between the *claim* to authority and the *response* to this claim, that ideological myths are deemed necessary to preserve the semblance of a united social consensus. (Such myths assure what Weber termed the 'charismatic' function of the social order.)

# V

Myth is an ideological function. But it is also more than that. Once a hermeneutics of suspicion has unmasked the alienating role of myth as an agency of ideological conformism, there remains the task of a positive interpretation. Hermeneutics thus has a double duty – both to 'suspect' and to 'listen'. Having demythologized the ideologies of false consciousness, it labours to disclose the utopian symbols of a liberating consciousness. This involves discriminating between the falsifying and emancipating dimensions of myth.

Symbolizations of utopia pertain to the 'futural' horizon of myth. The hermeneutics of affirmation focuses not on the origin (*arche*) *behind* myths but on the end (*eschaton*) opened up in *front* of them. It thereby seeks to rescue mythic symbols from the gestures of reactionary domination and to show that once the mystifying function has been dispelled we may discover genuinely utopian anticipations of 'possible worlds' of liberty and justice. A positive hermeneutics offers an opportunity to rescue myths from the ideological abuses of doctrinal prejudice, racist nationalism, class oppression or totalitarian conformism, and it does so in the name of a universal project of freedom – a project from which no creed, nation, class or individual is excluded. The utopian content of myth differs from the ideological in that it is inclusive rather than exclusive; it opens up human consciousness to a common goal of liberation instead of closing it off in the inherited securities of the *status quo*. We shall return to this point below.

Where the hermeneutics of suspicion construed myth as an effacement of some original reality (e.g. will to power, unconscious desire, the material conditions of production or domination), the hermeneutics of affirmation operates on the hypothesis that myth may not only conceal some pre-existing meaning but also reveal new horizons of meaning. Thus instead of interpreting myths solely in terms of a first-order reference to a pre-determined cause hidden behind myth, it discloses a second-order reference to a 'possible world' projected by myth. It suggests, in other words, that there may be an *ulterior* meaning to myths in addition to their

16

*anterior* meaning – an eschatological horizon which looks forward as well as an archaeological horizon which looks back. Myth is not just nostalgia for some forgotten world. It can also constitute 'a disclosure of unprecedented worlds, an opening on to other possible worlds which transcend the established limits of our actual world' and function as a 'recreation of language'.[26]

This *epistemological* distinction between the two horizons of myth (ie. archaeological and eschatological) also implies an *ethical* one. Myths are not neutral as romantic ethnology would have us believe. They become authentic or inauthentic according to the 'interests' which they serve. These interests, as Habermas recognized in *Knowledge and Human Interests* can be those of utopian emancipation or ideological domination. Thus the religious myths of a Kingdom of Peace may be interpreted either as an opiate of the oppressed (as Marx pointed out) or as an antidote to such oppression (as the theology of liberation reminds us). Similarly, it could be argued that the myths of Irish nationalism can be used to liberate a community or to incarcerate that community in tribal bigotry. And the same would apply to a hermeneutic reading of the Ulster Loyalist mythology of 'civil and religious liberties'. Moreover, our own century has also tragically demonstrated how Roman and Germanic myths – while not in themselves corrupt – have been unscrupulously exploited by Fascist Movements.

# VI

The critical role of hermeneutics is therefore indispensable. But this does not mean that we simply reduce mythic symbols to literal facts. It demands rather that we learn to unravel the concealed intentions and interests of myth so as to distinguish between their inauthentic role of ideological 'explanation' (which justifies the *status quo* in a dogmatic or irrational manner) and their authentic role of utopian 'exploration' (which challenges the *status quo* by projecting alternative ways of understanding our world). *Demythologizing,* as an urgent task of modern thought, must not be confused there with *demythizing* which would lead to a reductionist impoverishment of culture.[27] The crisis of modernity is characterised, in part at least by the separation of myth and history: a separation which led to the desacralization of tradition. But precisely because of this we need no longer be subject to the ideological illusion that myth *explains* reality. We should no longer expect myth to provide a true scientific account of our historical and geographical environment. "Demythologization works on the level of the false rationality of myth in its explanatory pretension".[28] Indeed it is the very demythologisation of myth in this sense which permits the rediscovery of myth as utopian project. Having eliminated the ideological function of explaining how things *are*, we are free to reveal the symbolic function of myth as an exploration of how things *might be*. We begin to recognize that the 'greatness of myth' resides in its ability to contain *more* meaning than a history which is, objectively speaking, true. This is what Ricoeur calls the 'saving of myth' through demythologization.

> We are no longer primitive beings, living at the immediate level of myth. Myth for us is always mediated and opaque . . . Several of its recurrent forms have become deviant and dangerous, e.g. the myth of absolute power (fascism) and the myth of the sacrificial scapegoat (anti-Semitism and racism). We are no longer justified in speaking of 'myth in general'. We must critically assess the content of each myth and the basic intentions which animate it. Modern man can neither get rid of myth nor take it at its face value. Myth will always be with us, but we must always approach it critically . . . Only then can we begin to recognize its capacity to open up new worlds.[29]

What is required, then, is a hermeneutic dialectic between a critical *logos* and a symbolic *muthos*. Without the constant vigilance of reason, *mythos* remains susceptible to all kinds of perversion. For myth is not authentic or inauthentic by virtue of some eternal essence *in itself*, but by virtue of its ongoing reinterpretation by each historical generation of each social community. Or to put it another way, myth is neither good nor bad but interpretation makes it so. Every mythology implies accordingly a *conflict of interpretations*. And this conflict is, in the final analysis, an ethical one. It is only when *muthos* is conjoined with *logos* in a common project of *universal* liberation for all mankind that we can properly speak of its utopian dimension. Whenever a myth is considered as the founding act of one particular community, to the total exclusion of all others, the possibility of ideological perversion immediately arises. Ricoeur makes this clear in the following passage from our discussion in *Dialogues with Contemporary Continental Thinkers:*

> The original potential of any authentic myth always goes beyond the limits of any single community or nation. The *muthos* of a community is the bearer of something which extends beyond its own particular frontiers; it is the bearer of other *possible* worlds . . . Nothing travels more extensively and effectively than myth. Whence it follows that even though myths originate in a particular culture, they are also capable of emigrating and developing within new cultural frameworks . . . Only those myths are genuine which can be reinterpreted in terms of liberation, as both a personal and collective phenomenon. We should perhaps sharpen this critical criterion to include only those myths which have as their horizon the liberation of mankind *as a whole*. Liberation cannot be exclusive . . . In genuine reason (*logos*) as well as in genuine myth (*muthos*), we find a concern for the *universal* emancipation of man.[30]

We best respect the universalist potential of myth by ensuring that its utopian *forward look* is one which critically reinterprets its ideological *backward look* in such a way that our understanding of history is positively transformed.[31] The proper dialectic of *muthos* and *logos* observes both the need to 'belong' to the symbolic representations of our historical past and the need to critically 'distance' ourselves from them. Without the critical 'distancing' of the *logos* we would not be able to distinguish between the ideological deformations of myth and its genuinely utopian promise. For *muthos* to guarantee its *u-topos,* it must pass through the purgatorial detour of *logos.* But a due recognition of our sense of 'belonging' (i.e. that our understanding always presupposes an historically situated pre-understanding) is also necessary; for without it critical reason may presume to possess an absolutely neutral knowledge beyond the limits of historical understanding. All objective knowledge about our position in a social community, historical epoch or cultural tradition presupposes a relation of prior belonging from which we can never totally extricate ourselves. The claim to total truth is an illusion. 'Before any critical distance, we belong to a history, to a class, to a nation, to a culture, to one or several traditions. In accepting this belonging which precedes and supports us, we accept . . . the mediating function of the image or self-representation'.[32] To renounce completely then the historical situatedness of the *muthos* is to lapse into the lie of a *logos* elevated to the rank of absolute truth. When reason pretends to dispense thus with all mythic mediations, it risks becoming a sterile and self-serving rationalism – an ideology in its own right which threatens to dominate our modern age of science and technology. Left entirely to its own devices, *logos* suspects everything but itself. And this is why the rational critique of myth is 'a task which must always be begun, but which in principle can never be completed'.[33]

# VII

We return, finally, to the crucial question of *national myth.* How may we demythologize tradition while 'saving its myths'? Here we are confronted with the hermeneutic task of discriminating between the ideological and utopian function of our national mythology. While it is absolutely essential to subject this mythology to a rigorous 'hermeneutic of suspicion' it would be foolish to conclude that all the myths of our tradition are reducible to the ideological function of mystification. We are obliged to respect the possibility that these myths contain a utopian horizon. As Tom Nairn rightly warns, even the most elementary comparative analysis shows that 'all nationalism is both healthy and morbid. Both progress and regress are inscribed in its genetic code from the start.'[34] Hence the limitations of the 'traditional Marxian negative hermeneutic for which the national question is a mere ideological epiphenomenon of the economic'.[35] In the 'political unconscious' of Irish nationalism there also exists a utopian project which it is unjust and unwise to ignore. But this utopian dimension of our national mythology is only ethically legitimate to the extent that it is capable of transcending all sectarian claims (i.e. to be the one, true and only ideology) in a universalist gesture which embraces those whom it ostensibly excludes. At a political level, one might cite here the readiness of the Forum for a New Ireland (to which all parties of Irish constitutional nationalism subscribed) to go beyond many of nationalism's 'most cherished assumptions' in order to respect opposing traditions and identities.[36] By thus demythologizing the myth of a 'United-Ireland-in-the-morning-and-by-whatever-means', it was possible to preserve the genuine utopian aspiration of the 'common name of Irishman' – a project which pledged to cherish all the children of the nation equally. At a literary level, we might cite the 'exploratory' narratives of James Joyce which demythologized the insularist clichés of Irish culture in order to remythologize its inherently universalist potential. Once a myth forfeits its power of ideological explanation, once it ceases to be taken literally as a force of hegemonic centralisation or domination, it ceases to mystify. And it is then, as Joyce reminds us, that its utopian mystery is revealed. Myth no longer serves as a monolithic doctrine to which the citizens of the nation submissively conform; it becomes instead a liberating 'bringer of plurabilities'. It is precisely the self-acknowledged *symbolic* nature of a myth's reminiscence and anticipation of collective harmony which commits it to a *multitude* of interpretations. 'In manifesting the purely symbolic character of the relation to men to the lost totality, myth is obliged to divide into multiple myths'.[37] The universality of myth is contained, paradoxically, in its very multiplicity.

Modern Irish culture provides us with many examples of this liberating multiplication of myth. The old Irish myth of Sweeney Astray has been reinterpreted in a wide variety of ways by poets such as Clarke and Heaney, playwrights such as Friel and MacIntyre, the novelist Flann O'Brien (in *At Swim Two Birds*) and the film maker, Pat Murphy (in *Maeve*). Far from constituting a recycling of some immutable national vision, these rewritings of the Sweeney myth manifest a rich variety of different and often conflicting narratives. The retrospective allusion to indigenous myth thus opens on to the prospective horizon of a more universal culture. It is because our modern consciousness no longer believes in myth – at an ideological/literal level – that we can reinvent myth at a symbolic/utopian level. Without disbelief there can be no 'willing suspension of disbelief'. Without demythologization, no remythologization.

But it is no doubt Joyce who most powerfully exemplifies this dialectic in his modernist rewriting of the national myth of Finn. *Finnegans Wake* invites us to have 'two thinks at a time' – for as the title itself informs us, this narrative refers both to Finnegan's *death* (the term wake in Ireland means a funeral ceremony) and to his *rebirth* (that is, Finn-again-awake). Joyce deconstructs the monolithic myth of Finn, the hero of Ireland's founding mythological saga, into an infinite number of myths. Joyce calls the *Wake* his 'messongebook'; and he thereby acknowledges that the 'national unconscious' – or the 'conscience of his race' as Stephen termed it – which expresses itself in his dreams *(mes songes)* of the legendary hero, may be interpreted either as an ideological lie *(mensonge)* or as a utopian cypher *(message)*. Joyce was clearly aware that the Celtic myth of Finn and the Fianna had been invoked by the Irish literary revival and by many of the leaders of the new Republic (whose most powerful national party was named *Fianna Fail)* in order to provide a renewed sense of cultural identity and unity for the Irish people. He saw the great potential of such myths as a means of animating the national unconscious. But he also recognized the possibilities of abuse. Joyce had little time for the sanctimonious romanticising which characterized aspects of the Celtic Revival. He disliked its tendency to turn a blind eye to the lived experience of the present out of deference to some sacralized fetish of the past. And he fully shared Beckett's disdain for a 'Free State' which proudly erected a commemorative statue of a dying Celtic hero in its General Post Office (where the Easter Rising began) at the same time as it introduced censorship laws which banned some of the finest works of its living writers. The recital of myths of the Motherland to legitimate a new intellectual orthodoxy was to be treated with critical scepticism; for such a practice was unlikely to foster a properly pluralist culture respecting the diversity of races, creeds and languages which existed in the nation. It was in defiance of chauvinistic stereotypes of the motherland that Joyce reinterpreted the ancient Celtic heroine, Anna, as Anna Livia Plurabella, whom he hailed as the 'Everliving Bringer of Plurabilities'. He thus opposed the 'one-mind' logic of ideological myth to the 'multi-mind' logic of utopian myth. *Finnegans Wake* features not *one* dominant personage but *many* interchanging personae who transform consciousness into a process of perpetual metamorphosis. Joyce's book explores not just one but many cultural myths (alongside the Celtic and the Judeo-Christian we find the Hellenistic, the Babylonian and the Chinese etc.). In both its form and its content, *Finnegans Wake* is a 'mamafesta' of multiple meaning.[38]

*Conclusion*

Joyce's literary model of myth as a creative 'bringer of plurabilities' has, I believe, immense implications for the reconciliation of traditions at both a political and religious level. It is not our purpose here to spell out these implications. Such a task surpasses both the limits of this paper and the competence of its author. Our task has been the more modest one of clearing some of the philosophical ground so that new debates might emerge. In conclusion, I can do no better than endorse Paul Ricoeur's recent plea that we "maintain the tension between tradition and utopia. For the problem is to reactivate tradition at the same time as we try to move closer to utopia."[39]

# NOTES

An amended version of this paper appears as Ch 8 of Richard Kearney, *Transitions* Dublin, Wolfhound Press 1987.

1. See in particular the structuralist and post-structuralist philosophies of Michel Foucault, Jacques Lacan and Jacques Derrida. For a detailed critique of this tendency see J.L. Ferry and A. Renault, *La Pensee 68: Essai sur l'anti-humanisme contemporain* (Gallimard, Paris, 1985). See Derrida's defence against such charges in my *Dialogues with contemporary Continental Thinkers,* Manchester University Press, 1984, pp. 123-126.

2. Karl Marx, *The Eighteenth Brumaire of Louis Bonaparte* (1852), Unwin Brothers, London, 1926. pp. 24-26.
   See also Ricoeur's definition of myuth in *Symbolism of Evil* Boston, Beacon Press, 1967, p.5.

3. See Terry Eagleton, 'Capitalism, Modernism and Post-Modernism' in *New Left Review,* No. 152, 1985, p.64; and also Walter Benjamin: *Towards a Revolutionary Criticism,* Verso, London, 1981. See also Ricoeur's discussion of this same relationship between critical innovation and tradition in Note 10 below.

4. Herbert Marcuse, *Eros and Civilization,* Beacon Press, Boston, 1955, p.19, and also Barry Katz, *Herbert Marcuse: Art of Liberation,* Verso, 1982,pp.102, 153.

5. Herbert Marcuse, *The Aesthetic Dimension,* Beacon Press, Boston, 1978, p.7.

6. Sean MacBride quoted in *The Cork Examiner,* 27th July 1985.

7. Frederic Jameson, *The Political Unconscious: Narrative as a Socially Symbolic Act,* London, Methuen, 1981. p.298.

8. Basil Chubb, *The Government and Politics of Ireland,* London, Longman, 1981, pp.21-23.

9. Dick Walsh 'Come on the Intellectuals' in *The Irish Times,* June 20 1985.

10. Walter Benjamin, 'Theses on the Philosophy of History' in *Illumination* Fontana, p.57. See also Paul Ricoeur, *Time and Narrative* (Vol.I), Chicago, Univ. of Chicago Press, 1984, pp.68-70.

11. Alasdair MacIntyre, *After Virtue,* London: Duckworth Press, 1981, p.206.

12. Séamus Deane, *Heroic Styles: The Tradition of an Idea,* Field Day pamphlets 4, Derry, 1984, p.18.

13. See Paul Ricoeur, *The Conflict of Interpretations,* Evanston, Illinois, 1974; *On Interpretation,* Yale, Yale University Press, 1970; and 'The Critique of Religion' in *The Philosophy of Paul Ricoeur: An Anthology of his Work,* ed. C. Regan and D. Stewart, Boston, 1978, p.215. See also 'Ricoeur's Hermeneutic Conflict' in *The Irish Philosophical Journal,* vol.2, No.11, pp.37.

14. Karl Marx and Frederick Engels, *On Religion* (Moscow, 1955), p.50.

15. Roland Barthes, *Mythologies,* London, Jonathan Cape, 1972.

16. Rudolf Bultmann, *The Theology of the New Testament,* SCM, London, 1952, pp.295f, and also Rudolf Bultmann and Karl Jaspers, *Myth and Christianity:* An Inquiry into the Possibility.

17. René Girard, *Le Bouc Emissaire,* Grasset, Paris, 1982 (in particular the chapter 'Qu'est-ce qu'un Mythe?' pp.36-37. See also my 'René Girard et le Mythe comme bouc émissaire' in *Violence et Verité': Colloque de Cérisy autour de René Girard,* Grasset, Paris, 1985, pp.35-49.

18. On this distinction between Utopia and ideology see Karl Mannheim *Ideology and Utopia,* London, Routledge and Kegan Paul, 1936; Frederic Jameson, 'The Dialectic of Utopia and Ideology' in *The Political Unconscious, op.cit.;* and Paul Ricoeur, 'Science and Ideology' in *Hermeneutics and the Human Sciences,* ed. J.B. Thompson, Cambridge, Cambridge University Press, 1981, pp.222-247.

19. Mircea Eliade, *Myths, Dreams and Mysteries,* London, Fontana, 1968, p.23: 'Myth is thought to express the absolute truth because it narrates a sacred history; that is, a transhuman revelation which took place in the holy time of the beginning . . . Myth becomes exemplary and consequently *repeatable* . . . By *imitating* the exemplary acts of mythic deities and heroes man detaches himself from profane time and magically re-enters the Great Time, the Sacred Time.'

20. Riceour, 'Science and ideology', *op.cit.,* p.225.

21. Riceour, *ibid.,* p.229.

22

22. Ricoeur, *ibid.*, p.227.
23. Ricoeur, *ibid.*, p.227.
24. See *Myth and Motherland*, Richard Kearney, Field Day pamphlets, 5, Derry, 1984 (republished in *Ireland's Field Day*, Hutchinson, London, 1985).
25. Jürgen Habermas, *Legitimation Crisis*, Boston, Beacon Press, 1973.
26. Paul Ricoeur, 'Myth as the Bearer of Possible Worlds' in *The Crane Bag*, Vol. 2, 1978; reprinted in my *Dialogues with Contemporary Continental Thinkers*, op.cit., pp.36-45.
27. On these distinctions between the 'explanatory' and 'exploratory' functions of myth and the critical procedures of 'demythologization' and 'demythizatrai' see Paul Ricoeur *The Symbolism of Evil*, New York, Harper and Row, 1967, and 'The Language of Faith, in *Union Sem. Quart. Review*, 28, 1973, pp.213-224; See also T.M. Van Leeuwen, *The Surplus of Meaning: Ontology and Eschatology in the Philosophy of Paul Ricoeur*, Rodopi, Amsterdam, 1981, pp.146-7.
28. Ricoeur, *The Symbolism of Evil, op.cit.* p.5.
29. Ricoeur, 'Myth as the Bearer of Possible Worlds', *op.cit.* p.39.
30. Ricoeur, *ibid*, pp.40-44. See also Mircea Eliade's perceptive account in *Myths, Rites and Symbols* vol.1, Harper, 1975, and in particular the sections on 'The Corruption of Myths' (pp.109-112) and on 'The Fallacy of demystification' (pp.120-123).
31. On this dialectic between ideology and utopia see my 'Religion and Ideology' *op.cit.* pp.48-50; also the section on 'mythe et logos' in my *Poetique du Possible*, Beauchesne, Paris, 1984, pp.190-198; and my interview with Ricoeur entitled 'the Creativity of Language' in *Dialogues with Contemporary Continental Thinkers*, op.cit. pp.29-30. Here Ricoeur suggests the possibility of a complementary dialectic between the retrospective horizon of ideology and the prospective horizon of utopia,

"Every society, as I mentioned earlier, possesses, or is part of, a socio-political *imaginaire*, that is, an ensemble of symbolic discourses. This *imaginaire* can function as a rupture or a reaffirmation. As reaffirmation, the *imaginaire* operates as an 'ideology' which can positively repeat and represent the founding discourse of a society, what I call its 'foundational symbols', thus preserving its sense of identity. After all, cultures create themselves by telling stories of their own past. The danger is of course that this reaffirmation can be perverted, usually by monopolistic elites, into a mystificatory discourse which serves to uncritically vindicate or glorify the established political powers. In such instances, the symbols of a community become fixed and fetishized; they serve as lies. Over against this, there exists the *imaginaire* of rupture, a discourse of *utopia* which remains critical of the powers that be out of fidelity to an 'elsewhere', to a society that is 'not yet'. But this utopian discourse is not always positive either. For besides the authentic utopia of critical rupture there can also exist a dangerously schizophrenic utopian discourse which projects a static future without ever producing the conditions of its realization. This can happen with the Marxist-Leninist notion of utopia if one projects the final 'withering away of the State' without undertaking genuine measures to ever achieve such a goal. Here utopia becomes a future cut off from the present and the past, a mere alibi for the consolidation of the repressive powers that be. The utopian discourse functions as a mystificatory ideology as soon as it justifies the oppression of today in the name of the liberation of tomorrow. In short, *ideology* as a symbolic confirmation of the past and *utopia* as a symbolic confirmation of the past and *utopia* as a symbolic opening towards the future are complementary; if cut off from each other they can lead to a form of political pathology."

32. Ricoeur, 'Science and Ideology', *op.cit.* 243.
33. Ricoeur, *ibid*, p.245; See also Ricoeur's study of the Habermas/Gadamer hermeneutic debate on this question in 'Hermeneutics and the critique of Ideology' in *Hermeneutics and the Human Sciences*, op.cit. pp.63-100. See my application of the *muthos/logos* dialectic to Irish culture in *Myth and Motherland*, Field Day pamphlets, 5, 1984.
34. Tom Nairn, *The Break-up of Britain*, New Left Books, 1977, p.348, (cited Jameson, *op.cit.* p.248).

35. Frederic Jameson, *The Political Unconscious,* op.cit., p.298.
36. See John Hume's opening address where he declared that the Forum was not a "nationalist revival mission" and that one of the reasons for our failure to resolve the national problem up to this may have been due to our inability to place the creation of a New Ireland "above some of our most cherished assumptions." *(Proceedings of the New Ireland Forum,* Vol.I, Dublin Castle, 1984).
37. Paul Ricoeur, *The Symbolism of Evil, op.cit.* p.168.
38. See the analysis of Joyce in my *Myth and Motherland, op.cit.* and in my 'Mythos und Kritik' in *Die Keltische Bewusstsein,* Dianos-Trikont, Munich, 1985.
39. Interview with Paul Ricoeur, *Le Monde des Livres,* 7th Feb. 1986.

# Reconciliation of Cultures: Apocalypse Now

*Séamus Deane*

The various attempts to reconcile the various ideas of culture in Ireland have been bound up with the requirements of different political situations. Oliver Mac-Donagh gives an account of one phase of this–from 1790-1820–in his book *States of Mind* (1983). The spectacle of men in holy orders engaging in disputes about pre-Christian Ireland, the better to establish the continuity of their own religious and political tradition with that era, has a certain piquancy. But it also demonstrates the tragic impossibility of their seeing any hope of establishing continuity between the separated religions and traditions of the contemporary period. History and culture are brought in to supply the deficiencies of the present. So Catholic resurgence in the late eighteenth century takes the cultural form of presenting the Gaelic past as a noble and ancient achievement, the inheritors of which no longer deserve to be deprived of civil life under the Penal system. Protestant reaction after 1800 takes the line that the Celtic past is of no consequence, that its recent resurrection is a piece of Romantic flimflam and that, therefore, Catholic claims to 'civility' are exaggerated or invalid. The story can be repeated with variations for the rest of the century and it extends, alas, into our own. Sir Samuel Ferguson, writing in 1833, appeals to the largely Protestant readership of the *Dublin University Magazine,* to "learn to live back in the country we live in"; his attack on James Hardiman's *Irish Minstrelsy* (1831) is the opening shot in his campaign to recover ancient Irish culture for the Protestant as well as for the Catholic Irish of the day, although the bigotry of his attitude towards Catholics tends to make his campaign seem less ecumenical in its implications than it actually was. So too, the Young Ireland movement, led by Thomas Davis, sought a Celtic foundation for all Irish sects and divisions by envisaging the Irish-English problem as a battle between Celtic Romantics and British Utilitarians, a theme which was to have a long run in Irish letters thereafter and was to supply writers as various as Yeats, O'Grady, Pearse and Matthew Arnold with the dominating element of their thought about Ireland.

Many of these efforts at cultural recovery and recuperation were promoted by people who, like Ferguson, O'Grady and Yeats, were trying to defend the interests of a class which was doomed to extinction to try, that is, to give, through culture, an extension of a life which had a diminishing political and economic future. Even when Catholicism became politically triumphant in twentieth century Ireland, we find various writers – Sean O'Faolain, Austin Clarke, Denis Devlin – attempting to reattach it to a European or to an ancient Irish past in order to rebuke and compensate for its narrow and philistine contemporary manifestations. In other words, culture has been used in Ireland for over 200 years (and arguably much longer) as a category in which the deficiencies of the existing state of affairs can be symbolically remedied. It is thus a compensatory activity, a displacement into one area of problems insoluble in another. Its history is both a dream of interpretation and interpretation of a dream. All through these various symbolic narratives we find that key-words – Celt and Saxon, Gaelic and Norman, Romantic and Utilitarian, English and Irish, Liberty and Freedom – are either haunted by or correlative with the basic disputatious religious terms, Catholic and Protestant.

To establish continuity is one thing; to do so in a triumphalist spirit, validating one tradition as authentic, others as spurious, is to reproduce the discontinuity the enterprise was designed to overcome in the first place. Whatever form our secular histories have taken – linear patterns of progress, cyclic patterns of rebellion against oppression, hypothetical patterns of what might have been or revisionist patterns dedicated to the exploding of all myths other than their own – it is surely true that no serious attempt has ever been made to see within our own history a pattern that could be described as essentially or structurally Christian, even though the story of Christian sects and their battles is an integral feature of our past and present. When I use the terms 'essentially or structurally Christian', I mean a mode of thought that is governed by the great historical typology of the Bible, one which has been more attractive to the artistic mind than to others. The seven phases of progressive revelation in the Bible have been described by the literary critic Northrop Frye as Creation, Exodus, Law, Wisdom, Prophecy, Gospel and Apocalypse. *(The Great Code,* 1982). I cannot pursue his account here. Variations of it can be found in some of the great masterpieces of the past – in Dante, Spenser and Milton – and in modern times, in Yeats and Joyce. Belief is not a precondition of being able to use the Bible although it sometimes seems to be a precondition of abusing it.

If we pause for a moment on the last phase, the Apocalypse, and its text, the Book of Revelation, we can elicit from it an example of the way in which we manage at regular intervals to use religion as a sanction for our failure or, indeed, refusal to reconcile cultures. Those seven-headed and ten-horned monsters, those dragons and horsemen, the Great Whore of Babylon and all the other allusions of the Old Testament which make up the fabric of that terrifying vision from Patmos, have been time and again used to ratify readings of history in which the downfall of the enemy – be it Catholicism, Protestantism, Communism or any other –ism – is foretold. This crudity is more often associated with Protestant fundamentalism than with any other sect, but it is true in a general sense that for many people, the Book of Revelation is an assurance that the truth, which is their truth, will prevail. This is exactly how one should not read a text of this kind. But it is also a lesson in how to create history as a story of eventual triumph. Misreading leads to rewriting, and the rewriting of the Book of Revelation is an outstanding example of the manner in which the Bible is recruited by Christians for sectarian and divisive purposes. As Northrop Frye points out in his discussion of Apocalypse, the Book of Revelation is not making a forecast, is not telling us that the great firework display is going to take place next Friday night or in the year 2000. Revelation, as the name implies, is an uncovering of what is happening now. It is a visionary formulation of the condition of our spiritual life. To read it as history is to suppress the spiritual, to make it subservient to the historical. The destruction described in Revelation is not the destruction of the world, but of man's exclusively secular vision of the world, the view which keeps us entrapped in time and space.

Mircea Eliade tells a story about a man who was collecting folk material in Yugoslavia in the 1950's. In one village, he heard a standard folk-tale about a young man who was about to be married to a local girl. Unfortunately for the young man, an enchantress had also fallen in love with him and tried to persuade him to give the girl up. He refused. As a consequence, on the night before his wedding, the enchantress lured him to a lonely cliff top and hurled him over to his death. If she could not have him, neither would her human rival have him. The collector asked when this had taken place and was astonished to hear that it had happened only sixty years before and that the bereft bride was still alive and still unmarried. He went to her and asked for her account. She told him that the death was an accident; that she and her betrothed were walking in the mountains above the village on the night before the wedding and he had slipped, fallen into a ravine and been killed. On talking to the other villagers, he was told differently. One account claimed that the bride was lying. She had killed her beloved herself because he had taken her to the mountains that evening to tell her that he was not going through with the marriage after all. Another version had it that the problem was political. The two lovers were separated by class and creed and that the man had finally bowed to his family's wishes and called off the marriage. For this she killed him. A variant on this was that he had committed suicide in despair and that his bride-to-be turned it into an accident to save her lover's name from the disgrace of suicide and to deny to the members of his family a triumph, however bitter, over her and him. Whatever the truth, the collector ultimately decided that the story of the enchantress was the only one into which all the others, so to speak, translated. She was a symbol, created by the people to explain the mystery of the man's death and also to take some of the harm out of it. It revealed a tragic truth but it obscured the actual facts which, in their divisiveness, could not but be damaging in repetition.

On an awesome scale, the Book of Revelation works like that folk story. It is a symbolic story, in code, of what is happening now. It tells of the great battles of repression, anxiety and fear, the collision between heaven and hell. The code can be read back into history. We can see it as the retelling of a battle between Croats and Serbs, Catholics and Protestants. But it is essentially a vision, not a myth. Used as a myth, it ratifies a version of history in which the forces of good overcome those of evil. There is a crucial, graded difference between, say, the Biblical metaphor of the saving remnant and Yeat's mutation of it into the idea of the elite, and Ian Paisley's version of it as the doctrine of the Elect and God's Chosen People. A powerful metaphor of that kind is lethal when it is understood as fact, most especially as a fact in history, not of history. In other words, it is a fact, in this light, which will be the end-product of history, towards which it yearns. There is in such readings a disguised teleology. They look forward to the day that is to come, to the extinction of those who prohibit its arrival. It denies the present for the sake of the future. It says we are trapped now but will be free later.

Such literalism dominates our thought. In Ireland, the translation into literalism is appealing because, given our historical circumstances, we turn to literature (more than to the other arts) to find there the reconciliations we find nowhere else in our political lives. But then we translate from the literature back into the irreconcilable categories in which we are incarcerated. Art tells us that we are both free and trapped, both now and forever. It is the history of the spirit to be caught in this endless dialectic. It is the history told by the Bible. When the Bible refers to language, it does so in terms of a famous metaphorical opposition. On the one hand, we have the confusion of tongues, represented by the Tower of Babel; on the other, we have the 'pure speech' promised to the restored Israel, the counterpart to the gift of tongues in the Acts of the Apostles. The Temple of Jerusalem touched heaven; the Tower of Babel tried to touch it. The Tower is the prison-house of language, the false structure, entirely secular. The Temple is Christ, who is the cornerstone. Cultures are a Babel that can only become a Temple when their languages become the pure speech that Israel was promised. The confusion of tongues creates chaos, the gift of tongues creates reconciliation. Christians, who should know this best, pay least attention to it. In this respect, artists are more essentially Christian than the religious.

Finally, it has to be asked why it is so difficult to achieve a reconciliation of cultures in this (or in any other) country. The kinds of story, the forms of translation, the species of literalism at which I have glanced seem to me characteristic of a culture (using this word in its broadest sense) which has not reached or which has lost its political maturity. A culture is not an entity which can safely or enduringly base itself upon the grounds of race or religion or territory. These are childish and dangerous concepts. They did have force, no doubt, at one time; but it is so long ago that it has almost passed out of mind. Unfortunately, since the nineteenth century, these concepts gained a new force and currency; in modern conditions, their effects were explosive. A mature culture is based on a political idea, not on racial essence, religious faith, or nostalgia for an historic territory. What Ireland needs is such a political concept. Neither that of the Republic nor that of the United Kingdom suffices any longer, because each is, by now, sectarianised. The Christian religions play themselves false if they assume their fate is bound up with the preservation of either. In doing so, they are mistaking the message of the Book of Revelation and misconstruing a political for a spiritual apocalypse. Religious literalism breeds political fanaticism and prevents the emergence of either a true conception of religion or the possibility of a true political idea. It would help the present situation if the distinction (not necessarily the separation) between Church and State were acknowledged by the Churches. Once admitted, then the Churches could again become part of our culture, rather than the translators of culture into literal and lethal politics.

# Reconciliation of Histories

*Margaret Mac Curtain*

The historian in a sense is the social psychologist of the past. He studies how individuals behave and what made them behave as they did; he studies groups of individuals, the interaction of groups, their growth, development and, in some cases, their dissolution. Unlike the psychologist, however, he finds no direct application in his discipline to human affairs, and few historians would claim that their knowledge of past events enables them to predict with any certainty the course of future events. On the contrary, it seems to imbue them with a more heightened awareness of the indeterminacy of human behaviour, with a greater insight into the transitoriness and relative instability of apparently solid and permanent institutions, and with a sense of the intransigence and paradox in human behaviour.

*Report of The Teaching of History in Irish Schools.*[1]

1966 was an important year of re-assessment of their historical past for Irish people. The national television station, RTÉ, carried a series of documentaries commemorating the fiftieth anniversary of 1916. Professor Francis Shaw wrote a powerful, immoderate article on 'The Canon of Irish History' – a challenge which seriously undermined the Pearse myth. Such was the mood of the time that the article was not published for six years. The study-group which presented the Report to the Minister of Education began in January 1966 and had ten sittings. The study group was chaired by Professor John Mc Kenna whose years of teaching and clinical experience in the field of child-psychology gave an added dimension to a group of seven people, four of whom had a professional interest in history. To one participant, looking back over a distance of some twenty years, the mind and influence of Professor T.D. Williams permeates the thinking expressed in substantial sections of the Report. Quintessentially, Desmond Williams was the historian of reconciliation. Notably in the fifties he guided students and readers of his reviews which appeared weekly in the pages of *The Irish Press*, and *The Leader* through the wastelands of historical positivism and placed them on the *terra firma* of historical objectivity. Invariably he directed the seeker to look for the purpose of history. History, he argued, is not what actually happened, but what historians, on the basis of available evidence (which is never complete), say has happened.

Section 5 of the Report, 'History Teaching for International Understanding and

National Identity' was, in the main, his contribution to the working party's deliberations. Here is in evidence his style of thinking aloud and his detachment to see as many sides of the problem as his researches enabled. Here too were expressed some of his favourite themes:

> While the fact that history should be used as a vehicle for promoting international understanding may not be universally accepted, there is little doubt that most people are agreed that history teaching should not be used to implant stereotypes, prejudices and irrational hatreds of other peoples. However, in our anxiety to minimise the irrational destructive forces which may be stirred up by strongly biased history teaching we should not make the mistake of being unduly evasive by suppressing the truth and modifying the facts in such a manner that they become meaningless. *p.282*

> Misunderstanding between nations, Professor Williams argues, falls into four categories. It is further exacerbated by prejudice and bias in history books and through teaching. The four categories enumerated are: 1. traditional international enmities between countries; 2. religious divisions between ethnic, social and national groups; 3. the assumption that western culture and civilisation and christianity, on which they are based, is the only culture and religion which is of value; 4. misunderstanding between ex-colonial powers and former subject nations giving rise to the conviction that white races are superior to all others. To former students of Desmond Williams this particular section of a long-forgotten Report puts them immediately in touch with his convictions about the nature of the historical process, and what the role of Irish history could become; indeed it is remarkable how much his philosophy has influenced the current debate on the true nature of 'revisionism' in Irish history.[2]

The middle years of the sixties were ones of relative security for society in the Irish republic. The visit of President John F. Kennedy of the United States to stay with President de Valera gave a fillip to a sense of being Irish in the wide world. The cordiality of the exchanges between the Taoiseach and the Prime Minister of Northern Ireland seemed to set the barometer at 'set fair'. The modest success of the republic's ambassadors at the United Nations was a visible indication of foreign policy incorporating and enchancing a real position on neutrality.

Twenty years later what is strikingly absent from that 1966 Report was an awareness of a need for some reconciling dimension in the relationship between the official history of the southern state and the development of Northern Ireland in the fifty years since 1916. The previous year a dialogue of north-south historians took place at Ballymascanlon outside Dundalk. The topic under discussion was that of 'Bias in the teaching of History'. The host planners were the committee of the European Society. To that dialogue came Professor J. C. Beckett of Queen's University Belfast and Professor T. D. Williams from University College Dublin.

Professor Patrick Lynch, the economist, took the chair on this occasion. How hopeful and vigorous it all seemed with three such distinguished 'reconcilers', speaking from diverse perspectives. Much of what J. C. Beckett said on that occasion is contained in his essay, 'The Study of Irish History' (*Confrontations: Studies in Irish History,* 1972). In that essay, as at the Ballymascanlon Dialogue Professor Beckett warned the student of Irish history to be prepared for an element of discontinuity in the study of the past. The history of Ireland can never be formulated simplistically as the struggle between native and foreigner. Nor can it ever be unified schematically in the mould of English or French history. Implicit in a scrutiny of England's past is 'a natural and overriding unity' which reaches back to the eleventh century. As for France, J. C. Beckett points out that there is a hierarchy of rank for national histories and French history is central to Europe and to the world as well as possessing patterns of unity and continuity.

The land of Ireland supplied the element of continuity, the matrix of all other relationships, in his estimation. Its influence on the inhabitants of the island was a thread that runs through the history of Ireland. Cogently he points out:

> But the writing of history can never be simply teleological; it is influenced, but not governed, by the end to which it moves; the process is more important than the conclusion. And to find any process of historical development that connects resistance to Anglo-Normans in the twelfth century with resistance to the Black-and-Tans in the twentieth, one must not only ignore the evidence that does exist, but invent evidence that does not exist. *p.16*

Not for nothing was J. C. Beckett's collection of essays entitled *Confrontations*. With inexorable logic he points out that for a large portion of settlers their relationship with Ireland remained ambiguous, and to a greater or lesser extent they resisted its influences in the realm of traditions and institutions, and in turn their ideas, tradition, and institutions profoundly influenced the earlier inhabitants of the island. He was, of course describing the settlers of that troubled century, the seventeenth, and his conclusions were indeed prophetic in the light of the violence that erupted in Northern Ireland after 1969. 'It is by studying the way in which the settlers were influenced by the conditions of Irish life, and the way in which they themselves modified the influence of those conditions in the earlier population, that we may well be able to identify the distinctive characteristics of Irish history, and build up a framework round which that history may be written.' *p.25*

Professor Desmond Williams approached the topic of bias from a different angle, that of a twentieth century historian with an intimate knowledge of Germany. Much of what he said was incorporated into the section he contributed to the Report the following year. The need for a continuous reassessment of possible prejudices in history teaching had resulted in the promotion of international studies of history teaching and a flow of textbooks. Notably after World War Two,

Unesco had endeavoured to set up an exchange between French and German historians. The 1951 Unesco Commission on the teaching of history for international understanding instructed historians to examine such areas to which the attention of teachers should be drawn in order to bring their teaching into concord with the facts established by scientific research. In the sixties there were courageous attempts to produce a 'European' textbook: in these attempts the European schools which accompanied the growth of the consciousness of the European Community reported on their limited success, limited mainly because of the retention of traditional prejudices and interpretations. Prejudice, according to Desmond Williams, was the single most obstinate element which impeded the progress of modern research from filtering down into the textbooks. With prejudice can be associated the magnetic attraction of stereotypes.

Can histories be reconciled? Is truth so harsh that it threatens with fragmentation the illusory reality which in a multiplicity of fragile structures envelopes, not just our personal identity but the past identities of our communities? Does the seemingly unassailable fortress of each particular establishment on this island, Unionist or Republican, Protestant or Catholic, remain impervious to the persuasion of rational analysis of our shared past? Specifically now, at this point of time, what is the position of the founding myths of the modern state(s) of Ireland?

Identity is at the core of reconciliation. Crucial to an understanding of our present *impasse* is the realisation that the inability to discard those elements of a national identity which make it a caricature and even grotesque identi-kit leaves the communities on this island in a kind of trapped stasis. There is, for instance, the top-of-the-morning, beer-swigging, stage Irishman who has been with us a long time, the 'fictional' Irishman, a construct whose nationality poses no threat to the ethnic divisions that run through Irish society.[3] More subtle in ways is the ultra-nationalist whose defensiveness against the outside world is an assertion of anti-English sentiments, one who balances Gaelic antiquity against the English intruder, Gaelic spirituality against materialism from outside the island, and whose 'national' literature is a form of alienation of the colonised.

There is, then, a high degree of integrity demanded of the historian who makes the decision to retain processes of reflecting, writing and presenting Irish history in the first language of the state, Irish, aware that, as the twentieth century draws to a close, this is to render him speechless to whole sections of the population of the island, and not listened to by groups who profess to think and speak in Irish. It is a predicament not unknown to the Dutch historian, Pieter Geyl. In his essay, 'The National State and the writers of Netherlands History' he examines the conflict that arises between the history of a linguistic group, Flanders, which is at least potentially a national group, and the modern states established in that area, Belgium and the Netherlands. Geyl considers the ability of the nation states to change their attitudes as an important factor in bringing about unity: 'the Catholics now pull their full weight both in the political and cultural life of Holland. The Protestant conception of Dutch nationhood, which had been decaying for so long already, has become frankly untenable. Meanwhile in Belgium the Flemish Movement obtained the redress of most of the old grievances'.[4] Geyl's conclusions are as valid for Ireland today as they were for the Netherlands after World War Two, in the final paragraph where he speaks so tellingly of the historian's obligation to be aware of the existence of a problem. It is that of the mind-set which allows no freedom to cross 'the boundary of one's sentiments or prejudices' and, adds Geyl, it has often been fostered by the modern state 'with its high claims to total allegiance, and with its efficient machinery to assist, but at the same time gently to guide, the historian'.

History as an academic discipline in Britain and Ireland is over a hundred years old if we accept Ranke and Acton as its founders. In that span of over a century little acknowledgement has been gestured towards the changing role of memory, or indeed towards the impact of psychology on our understanding of memory, and how it works. Despite our growing dependence upon information systems and our recognition of the computer-like components of the human memory, at times it appears as if popular Irish history functions in a mysterious continuum that has more in keeping with the storing capacity of the bardic memory of four hundred years ago than it has with the Unesco recommendations on the teaching of history to young people. One of the contemporary movements of today's historians is to be interested in the cluster of attitudes and psychological traits that create a mentality, or a collective mentality within different levels of a particular society. We are a memory-carrying people who know all the tricks of keeping race-memories alive through song, music and ballad.

> And one read black where the other read white, his hope
> The other man's damnation:
> Up the rebels, to Hell with the Pope
> And God Save – as you prefer – the King of Ireland
>
> *Louis MacNiece 1938*

Historians in the mid-eighties are asking (and endeavouring to answer their own questions) if there is a general *Weltanschauung* or collective set of attitudes which remains obdurate to any imposition of formal, conscious beliefs and constitutes a certain temper or mentality.[5] Memory as history was 'invented' by Renaissance humanism and developed as a handmaid of the emerging nation-states of Europe in the following centuries. Machiavelli's reflections on the connection between history and power suggested that history could be made by an act of resolution on the part of the ruler. He also implied that the spoils of victory gave to the victor the right to render the 'official' history and thus please the Prince. As for the vanquished, they retained their memories and out of them narrated their own version of what happened, passing it on orally to future generations in a variety of media.

We go to history, as to economics – where formerly we went to religion or the classics – to find a meaning for life. Each generation has then an obligation to write its own history. But first memories need to be reconciled. Hurt memories cry out for healing. Distressful memories can keep a myth like Ulster's Bloody Massacre of 1641 trapped in a dismal recurring record. One way to deal with an uncomfortable past is to carry out an operation on the brain, to anaesthetize the pain of the past. One way of presenting Irish history is to execute some kind of cosmetic alteration on its face, to clean up those sad, dark places where the human spirit droops from the weight of its history, and offer a bland synthesis of the 'good old times'. But this kind of forgetting or deliberate disremembrance is to render Ireland's past a kind of leprechaun land, or if we are dealing with the twentieth century, a Disneyland. The sanitization of Irish history, what a theme for a futuristic television series!

'National memories and ideological instincts cannot be disregarded' was according to Desmond Williams, axiomatic for the direction of foreign policy on the part of governments.[6] Equally he could have placed the Irish Civil War in that context. An authority on the Irish civil war, he once lectured for two hours and twenty minutes on that topic holding an audience comprised of survivors, diplomats, people who had not spoken to each other for over a quarter of a century. When he had finished in an atmosphere of hushed silence the applause that broke out was tumultuous. More important for the historian his objectivity and fairmindedness were commended. With that lecture there commenced a new era of approaching Ireland's recent past in history writing. A path-breaking series of radio lectures on the years between Easter 1916 and the first years of the new Irish state, edited by T. D. Williams, made their appearance in book-form in 1966. it was titled *The Irish Struggle* and within its covers were a collection of well-researched essays by leading experts. There for the first time readers had access to the Williams' analysis of the Irish civil war.[7]

The eruption of violence in Northern Ireland since 1969 has long since shattered any complacency the Irish republic may have experienced fifty years after the 1916 Rising. The task of writing recent Irish history has not been easy over the last twenty years. In the eighties a new reproach was hurled at those historians who were engaged in writing political history of the twentieth century; they were 'revisionists' and they wrote 'revisionism', not history.

It is a word that has not yet found its place in the 1985 edition of *The Oxford Dictionary of current English;* nevertheless it is a word that has found currency among journalists, students and readers of *The Irish Post*. It is too soon to assess the consequences of the hostility that the writing of Irish history by a younger generation has provoked, or to gauge the effect of the word 'revisionism' in terms of linguistic evolution. If the usage persists and leads to clarity and accuracy, then it will ultimately facilitate the writing of history; if on the other hand, 'revisionism' is used as a term that fudges or obfuscates significant areas of historical understanding, we must conclude that unconscious assumptions are getting in the way of receiving correct information.

Sometimes it is not prejudice that freezes people into a mind-set, it is fear. The 'crime' of Galileo was that he proposed for consideration an obvious truth, that the earth is not the centre of the universe; he challenged an article of faith, one upheld by Church and State, shrouded in tradition, rooted in language. The myth-level of a society has a volcanic dimension, however deeply embedded in the unconscious it appears to be. In a sense both Dr Richard Kearney and Professor Séamus Deane rendered the topic under consideration here, 'Reconciliation of Histories', a service when they drew our attention to the myth element in a culture. Is it possible to demythologise national myths and yet preserve the country's myths? To put it more starkly, can myths become conduits of destruction that necessitate demolition?

From time to time there sweeps over practitioners of the craft of Irish history feelings of being maimed or scarred by our history. It remains disconcertingly present below the surface. With it goes as a nagging accompaniment a sense of being 'losers' in the panorama of world history. Some countries have similar wounds, Poland, the Lebanon, Mexico. To possess a history of discontinuity is no disgrace. Meaning and pattern are concealed in that discontinuity. What matters is not the validity of the question: why did our history happen this way or that, but what role has our memory played in keeping us victims of our past, or inheritors of our future?

## NOTES

1. Report on The Teaching of History in Irish Schools, *Administration,* Vol. XV (1967) pp. 268-85.
2. The author is indebted to the late Professor T.D. Williams who suggested a re-examination of the Report in the light of the Ballymacscanlon Dialogue. His untimely death prevented further discussions with him on the theme. The weakness in this paper are mine, the illuminatoins his.
3. For an interesting development of this idea, cf. J.T. Leerssen, *Mere Irish & Fíor-Ghael,* Amsterdam., 1986, pp. 85-168.
4. P. Geyl, *Debates with Historians,* London Fontana, 1962, pp. 228-9.
5. See, for example, G.E. Aylmer, 'Collective Mentalities in mid-seventeenth century England: The Puritan outlook' in *Royal Historical Transactions,* Fifth Series, No. 36, London 1986, pp. 1-25.
6. T.D. Williams, 'The Primacy of Foreign Policy' *Nonplus* 2, 1960, unpaginated. I am grateful to my colleague, Dr. Michael Laffan, History Department, U.C.D. for having drawn my attention to this seventeen-page essay.
7. Further to Civil War archives and the Thirty Year rule see R. Fanning, '"The Great Enchantment"; uses and abuses of modern Irish history', pp 136-7 in *Ireland in the Contemporary World. Essays in honour of Garret Fitzgerald ed* J. Dooge, Dublin, Gill and Macmillan, 1986.

# Reconciliation as Remembrance
## "It takes two to know one"

*Joe Harris*

### Introduction

The humanist project, the western tradition of rationalism in its various forms, which we are all heirs to whether we like it or not, is a project of self assertion. It is carried forward on a number of presuppositions which it has taken us several centuries to even begin to see clearly, and we are well into another in the work of reconsideration and reconstruction of its implications. The major presupposition is that as human beings we have one task and that is self-preservation; but the human being referred to is a self, a knowing subject who is assumed to be motivated by the necessity to dominate and master both internal desire and external 'nature'. A sense of subjectivity comes about paradoxically through the disciplined repression of the anarchic desire for happiness, accomplished not just as a private venture, but through cultural forms, in particular the institutions of 'knowledge'. The self which is created and promoted through this cultural complex is the human subject of *knowing*.[1] This culture of knowing rests on an approved division (in which theory and practice are at one) between the knowing subject and the world as object.

A second feature of the enlightenment project is the generation of theories of 'language'[2] which support and embody the first major epistemological assumption. It has been bolstered by the philosophy of consciousness, some of the breaches in which have been exposed yet again in crisis, this time that of consumer capitalism.

### The Demise of the Humanist Project

The demise of the humanist project, we might now say, is not unexpected given the contradictions set up between self society and the thrust to maintain communicative structures which, in evolutionary terms, fuels change and, in Christian terms, is the work of redemption in creation. Although mediated by 'knowledge' of God and having a name the self is erased through the very logic of the project.

> Through the presentation of a consistent narrative of personal experience, the subject seeks to establish individual identity and to secure personal property. Such self-presentation is inseparable from recollection, representation and repetition. The temporality of the subject, however, subverts the identity, propriety, presence and property of selfhood. This subversion effectively dispossesses the subject.[3]

It is not unexpected given the Faustian core, and in the case of atheistic humanism it is a

> . . struggle for domination (which) embodies the interrelated principles of utility and consumption which lie at the heart of technological consciousness. The psychology of mastery and the economy of domination represent efforts to deny death. This labour proves to be both narcissistic and nihilistic. Such self-assertion is finally *self*-defeating.[4]

We shall return to this question of how recollection, representation and repetition are linked and how 'memory' is subverted.

The inner meaning of the humanist project, as it has been exposed in its social forms, has been challenged in their different ways by Marx and his followers, by Weber particularly in his identification of the process of rationalization, and by the Frankfurt tradition[5] which has explored the disillusionment of the age at the dominance of instrumental reason. The intellectual and practical challenge thrown down by these analyses have been picked up by a growing critical sociological tradition.[6]

### A Postmodern Context?

Are we in a post-modern age?[7] The sense of the breakup of orthodoxies in one way is stronger than it has ever been.[8] There is a play of discourses, few of which can listen to each other. In his analysis of a particular example, Castoriadis[9] describes a culture which is a symptom:

> . . a culture which aims at (and largely succeeds in) dividing everything between the algorithmic and the ineffable, between pure 'machine' and pure 'desire', and which drives into exile or makes unthinkable the essential core of what we are and what matters to us.

Some regenerate the possibility of subjectivity (however anonymous) in cybernetic dreams, while others despair and plan to retreat from urban and social decadence either to the isolation and seclusion of the survivalists' wilderness or to the communal security of mindless affirmations of rightness and righteousness against the worldly legions of the devil. There is still plenty of life left in the fundamental desire as can be seen from ever renewed versions of the 'problematic individual' (Lukacs). One of the things that should concern us is the failure to communicate between all those who sense the distress of our accumulated history, on one side those who are still committed to the enlightenment project and on the other those who are claiming to dissociate themselves from its premises[10] and trying to be critical without being self-righteous – exceedingly difficult it must be admitted when so many forms of intellectual discourse are captured by the intellectual and political commitments of the university.

It makes all the difference whether or not we feel the failure of the

Enlightenment project, the domination of instrumental reason that is structured into our culture as competitiveness and consumption. Perhaps all of us to one degree or another live with "a reified consciousness, comfortably adjusted to its alienation",[11] and we all share in Hugo Ball's feeling that

> this humiliating age has not succeeded in winning our respect.[12]

To regenerate subjectivity will involve a break with accepted tenets of what reason is through a restructuring of what we mean by thought and feeling, and a struggle to recover the wisdom of the notion that

> Man is not an essentially intellectual creature.[13]

## Reconciliation as Transgression

In this context I think that reconciliation will mean 'transgression', for reconciliation is not about the repression of difference, but about us jointly transgressing the constraints, the boundaries that have solidified into our precious 'differences'. However we would not be holding on to our differences and our boundaries did we not 'think' that it was worth the trouble. Experience suggests therefore that however joyful this transgression will become in our maturity, it will at first restimulate old fears and old distresses. To accomplish this task we need to recover 'memory' from the reductionist versions which hold sway in cybernetics and linguistics, let alone everyday speech. It seems to me to be fundamentally mistaken to conceive of memory as the capacity to recall and recollect things and events. We never do that, first because there is nothing there of that order to recollect and because recollection is not the name of the game. That is the postivist account of 'memory' structuring the activity of 'recollection'. What we have lost is the experience of constructing narratives, as a *shared* practice in the 'present'. In its place we have substituted descriptions which dissociate 'us' from the 'event'. It will therefore not be easy

> restoring judicious memory to its rightful place in the conversation of culture.[14]

Something essential to our self-understanding as human beings is connected to the notion of memory; it is the pivot of culture.[15] Equally impressive is the rigid and repetitive force exerted against creativity by memory as deep cultural patterns of experience and language which we seem unable to steer. This volume provides insights into this, in particular the distortions involved in (but not caused as such) by the class of relationships referred to as those of collective responsibility. The distortions are the expression in cultural forms of the battle between unacknowledged memories and public remembrances. The question then becomes whether we are to be stuck with memories (and more memories) or can we engage in cultural remembrance which does not simply reactivate old rivalries and open old wounds.

The subtitle of this chapter comes from Gregory Bateson.[16] It reinforces the claim that there can be no 'cheap' reconciliation, for it challenges the assumption that knowing myself starts from a knower and works outwards in increasing rings of intersubjectivity. The proposal is that coming to know, if it is not to be the fractured epistemology of rationalism just outlined, is based on a relation, a connection, not simply between the knower, and the known but in the wider context of knowing between connected knowers.[17] One of the most exciting intellectual moves to have taken place over the last forty years has been the recognition that, however astonishing the exploration of 'nature' by what was defined as experimental 'observation', when we look at living and cultural systems or move to the microscopic level we are into the realm of what Prigogine and others have called *autopoiesis*.[18] The characteristic of such analysis is that it gives a central place to the fact that systems are self-observing.[19] Of course they always have been, and much in philosophy and social theory for a long time has been saying just that. The space that has cleared now is based on recognizing the nature of systems limits (a good example is Godel's work on undecidability[20] and its disastrous implications for mechanistic systems thinking) and that we do not have to pretend to be able to step outside a system to be able to observe and be critical. The validity of our 'observations' does not depend on that assumption about knowing. It is simply radically different from how traditional science knows about (indeed creates) its world. From this point of view consciousness[21] takes on a different meaning as it moves from a knowing based on 'objectivity' to knowing based on participation. The validity conditions change as they find a basis in the nature of communication, but in order to make this move we have to be clear that communication is not reduced to cybernetic information processing. Central to this approach is a reconsideration of what we mean by 'memory'.

In this context we are talking about reconciliation of people, subjects as embodied experience, and not just historical revisionism. Reconciliation as communication between subjects has to encompass the substance and the import of objective accounts open to rational inquiry. Hence I find that I can no longer be satisfied just with the recovery and rewriting of 'Irish' history as if that would take care of and reconstruct memory. What I want is something more fundamental which is heralded in the language of reconciliation.

*The Economy of Experience — Being Protestant in Ireland*
How did I come to this position? I was brought up in the part of Belfast known as Sandy Row, and its extension into what is now called (but was not in my childhood) The Village. This set of connections gave me structured, but as I shall claim, contradictory accounts of the world. One of these is the basic Unionist-and-Protestant ideology that we (read: no 'I' without a 'We') live in a set-up the fundamental rightness of which is implicit in all we think. Anyone who would dare to question this could only be in process of losing their wits. This is fitted into the

language we use every day and into the attitudes we are encouraged to adopt. I say fitted into language because there is a niggling sense of incompleteness, a hiatus, like a little wound, just enough to be troubling without being disabling, between the flow of experience and the managed 'use' of language. It is reinforced in my case by being brought up also in the Gospel Hall,[22] in which the bible from Genesis to Revelation is presented every day as the 'text' (and in this business 'texts' are vital) whose imagery interprets all memory and will therefore provide all I need to make sense out of the world now and to come.

Alongside this patterning of my life there is what I want to call 'experience'. At some level, I was experiencing something quite different which was constantly cutting across the account and the ideology presented to me as the one I should hold on to if I wished to retain a sense of family connections and to know who 'I' was. Part of this sense of cross-cutting experience was fed by the very evidence called in to support the ideology of biblical unionism. The whole of the biblical canon is offered as an indivisible unity not open to fancy interpretation and individual picking and choosing, since the interpretation that does away with the need for further interpretation has been done.[23] However there are parts of this total story which, when read through the very 'Protestant' codes of language which were thought to have created and to buttress the 'correct' reading, keep running up against the public account of how I should feel and what values I should place on people and ideas.

To a person who has language (and the structure of mediation somehow forgot this) there are bits of the hallowed text which constantly disturb the monolithic version of life supposedly based on the text and the approved reading. I live therefore in a world in which I am enabled by some of the very resources which created the orthodoxy to challenge it. It certainly made life confusing and uncertain, but nudged me to pursue the valued but also dangerous thing which big people hinted at in talk about thinking for yourself. At this distance I can only think that they were warning of the sense of isolation and fear that went with anything as dangerous as thinking, and it took me a long time to realize that many of them had indeed been impelled into this fearsome activity but had got stranded and given up, at least temporarily, rather than risk being cut off as they must have imagined from their birthright. It will take just a little imagination to picture what it was like living in Belfast, at a time when there was nothing like the rigid housing segregation that there is now, where you live close to people who are supposed to be of a different ilk from you, to think differently about the world, to look different (though you look for the evidence you can find none), people whom you meet and together with whom you get on with fundamental things like playing games – until some crisis arises, or someone uses a particular word that sets the whole thing awry. I took it for granted that this was what the real experience of life was somehow about for everyone. In retrospect it feels appropriate to say that I was fed

41

by that experience. I assume it places me, as it does every one else who reflects on the contradictions and connections in their life, in a situation where there is a gap between the public accounts through which the culture is negotiated and my experience as a subject which invites me (almost irresistibly) to start rewriting the accounts. It never occurred to me that political theorists might define my life as a narrow one, locked in what they patronizingly call the usual banalities of everyday life. The present volume is about resisting that despairing stance.

## Time for Finding Language

When we lived perpetually on the edge of crucial definitions about the categories through which 'identity'[24] is structured, the question which kept coming up then was what was I going to do with this discomfort. A number of routes were offered to me, partly in the process of a 'liberal' education. The first was that I should find a different language with which to work. In this regard I need to say a little here about language and then later to develop the issue of language and memory. I feel it overstates the issue to say that language is all we have to keep us critical and aware. Language is crucial but is not itself the context. For that, communication is needed, the material context in which to string together forms of language in terms of information, utterance and understanding. The danger is that we think of language in terms of a self-contained system that is opposed to the world.

> Expression is possible because its extra-linguistic correlate belongs to the world; if the referents were not connected, there could be no connection among the signifiers of language . . . The organization of language is always based upon the organization of the world, for it necessarily rests upon what is invisible in the visible.[25]

This quotation is an elaboration of ideas of Merleau-Ponty, [26] who had a strong sense of the relation between world and word and of the nature of language. The following paraphrases him:

> But it is also language itself that is expressed in expression. The being of language and the being-thus of language are expressed in every word of that language.[27]

Language is not a container of set meanings but the generator and carrier across seemingly impossible boundaries. Merleau-Ponty spoke of language being about 'parts' but each part was paradoxically a

> total part . . . representative of the whole, not by a sign-signification relation, or by the immanence of the parts in one another and in the whole, but because each part is *torn up* from the whole, comes with its roots, encroaches upon the whole, transgresses the frontiers of the others.[28]

A relation of the world and the word of this order releases us from the tyranny of a language digitalized and subordinated to ideas or 'reality' but equally from the view of language as our evolutionary talisman without which we would be dumb brutes. Either of these is to de-mean language and may help to explain why sincerity of intent, when based on faulty assumptions about the limits of language, has not proved a safeguard against the disintegration of reconciliation work.

Trying out different language meant that I had avoided the question of 'language'. All my 'languages' left me short of the point where I could grapple with the experience of hiatus, the missing bits, the knowledge of an erasure, a rupture, but also of access, of invitation, even of plenitude and of the possibility of integration and restart. As I see it now this was being intimated in everyday language. The blocks are not inherent in the system of language communication and relations. They are identifiable in a particular cultural network and in the systems of subjective meaning through which social structure is managed by me the person. It is such a relief to discover that this management is not controlled, though it is influenced, by the concepts inscribed in the social and psychic structure through which we each make do at any given time.

*Writing an Uncensored History*
A second route to resolve the contradiction between experience and cultural meanings was to learn more about the history, recover the censored facts. Then I would find encouragement to reach a consensus of some sort with those who differed from me. (At this stage it is easy to see that difference is treated as a problem rather than a resource). This is surely an important task, for one way to release the imagination is to make available more of the social historical text in which consciousness is rooted. This 'text' is created in the actions of local times and places but the connections across time surpass these original actions and structure new patterns that are beyond the intentions of the original actors.[29] The gaps and blanks one comes across can be startling – at least from the point of view of the observer whose consciousness communicates with different gaps. A student whose family, religion and schooling in the cultural context of the north of Ireland would lead one to assume particular knowledge had not at the age of 20 heard about Daniel O'Connell. Discussion on the problems of teaching Irish history led to the student going home and asking parents why they had told their selection of Irish history. The story becomes more confused at this point because it is not clear whether or not 'information', let's call it, was available in school or whether the message from 'home' was to steer clear of controversial issues, disengage from a contentious history for the sake of a supposed freedom from bias and indoctrination.

Parents appear to say they don't want to do to children what was done to them, that is set them up able to see the world only one way, enclose them in a language which cuts them off from other narratives and interpretations. It was an

43

understandable mistake for parents to make; it was based on assumptions which a serious practice of reconciliation would have to challenge. The erroneous assumption is that by using a particular language we risk being trapped in the concepts, ideas and thought patterns which are used as the knowledge commodities of a rationalistic culture. This mistake derives from treating language as a conscious system, parts of which can be avoided as if contaminated, rather than the less instrumental version I have sketched above, in which human beings continue to create the world and the word – and therefore memory.

### Total Parts

At some point I came to the conclusion that it was not enough to work at retrieving the uncensored (rather than complete) history of our relations in the island of Ireland, however an important aspiration that is. Neither the search for a history nor a more sophisticated language could handle what was around – indeed they exacerbated the situation. For, travelling around Ireland I find I am confronted by an experience of pain which I have come to interpret as being in touch with the experience of *the past* (that is what our language invites us to say), what is beyond my time available in my time, an example of Merleau-Ponty's *total part*. The very act of looking on the land imaginatively and listening releases feeling which is this person, me, registering what *is*. It is not mystification in language or the fantasies of an observer projected unto an objectified world. When I became aware that I was being confronted by this kind of evidence that needed some kind of translation I knew where to turn. It was to the messages that I recalled hearing long ago but did not know what to do with. I made the connection a couple of years back on the Twelfth of July at the 'field' in Garvagh, Co. Derry, when I held on to my painful connection with all the people around me, and accepted that the same disturbance had happened when as a child[30] I used to go to the Orange parades and to the old field at Finaghy and could not understand my bond and my disconnection, or (as I thought) struggle to disconnect. What I had resisted all those years was a recognition of the intertwining of all the history of this land, the interlacing times of history[31] and the contradictions and confusions that must follow when we attempt to screen out these connections for the sake of a manipulable history. What I had to accept was that in a creative sense the history held me and that I needed to get out of the rivalry with its capacity to transcend me, and find out where there were resources to help. The crucial step was to see that we cannot recover memories as if there were such things. We can do something qualitatively different.

### A Remembrance Version of Memory

The resource explored in this volume is a systemic version of memory, bringing remembrance back into the story as something more than the mere recall of information from the computing device in the head. Habermas talks, in the particular context of our understanding of 'science', of the need to

> . . . deliberately marshall the analytical power of remembrance against those forces of repression in which scientism finds its roots,[32]

as part of a more extended programme of retrieving effaced aspects of our how we let ourselves know and the difficulty of admitting a central place to self-reflexion (sic).

It would not be surprising if many find this kind of talk confusing, given the kind of world we are faced with – one dominated by narrow rationalistic assumptions about thought and feeling. Some of us would write this kind of experience out of the story as a grand pathetic fallacy, a projection of 'personal' experience into an impersonal world. It would be a pity if we did this because it will obstruct the work of reconciliation by restricting the range of what has to happen. It would be possible for the work of reconciliation of memories to be displaced through glib formulae or set apart from subjective experience in an alienated way, because we must keep our rational feet on the ground. I too aim for that but what I mean by rational is different, and have tried to indicate something of what that is. It comes as a bit of a shock to have to give up the implied (but never very substantial) control of the thinking person in the way that it has been promoted through the liberal values that inform our education systems, in which we 'think' a lot about literature and art and display conceptual dexterity but feel little. Witkin reflects a widely shared point of view when he says:

> The repression of subjectivity in our own age . . . has made of subjectivity a topic of special attention and study. This is all the more so because in the severe objectification of our existence the repression has taken a peculiar form. We have not denied the claims of feeling. On the contrary, we have solemnly endorsed these claims. Our problem is that we have forgotten what they are. The task of remembering must begin again in earnest . . .[33]

The resources are of course there for it, but the struggle, which is about re-evaluating the presuppositions of the enlightenment through which the culture is meditated, is resisted with both reason and innuendo. The visual arts, music, literature can leave us superficially ruffled, but there will be no new dream material, no stirring of the imagination, no experience of seeing, no excitement through the interrogation of appearances.[34]

Can we deliberately go about promoting the work of remembrance? I look back at myself and say that it was premised on holding on to the uneasiness and indeed queasiness of everyday life. It is helped along by actively filling in gaps, enlarging the horizon of vision by listening to the voices of the world– many of which we have to read off as confused and disillusioned, as part of a pact to narcotize us, and as deep cultural distresses projected into the structure of our everyday lives. But other voices we should talk with, harmonize with, though there is no code book to tell us which. Reconciliation is intimate with these issues, both listening in general and the particular voices in our bodies which are the available evidence of our cultural condition. Once we assume that reconciliation is about world and word, and that this is possible only if we reject the rigid separation of analogic and digital modes of communication,[35] we will always be struggling with amorphous, shapeless sentiments (not phantasies in the sense that the notion is used in psychoanalysis). This is what all our attempts at naming are about – the task of shifting the line between the conscious and the unconscious, which is imperative if we are to redeem the claim to subjectivity inscribed in our being separate in a social world. This range of feeling we cannot name too soon. Reconciliation appears to involve a commitment to *finding* language to talk to one another about experience and not look for shortcuts to knowing and naming.

### The Data of Remembrance

A starting point would be the acknowledgement (in whatever form it would take), in face to face meetings where the trace of our history can only be avoided, that the history of this (these) island(s) is written in the bodies of all the human beings (other life forms I cannot consider here) who happen to be, or have been, living on the island(s). As for the time scales involved I can only make a guess. It took me a long time to discover that I didn't live with just the particular selection of history that had been handed on to me as if it were from the outside. I came to realize that the history was revealed in its very delivery as partial, and that the strain of living was generated in the making of the narrative, because the assumptions about history did not acknowledge the complexity of experience, principally because the conception of language kept suppressing the analog dimension of experience. Koselleck seems to me to be on the right tack but is stuck with a distinction between linguistic and extralinguistic dimensions of experience.

> In the absence of linguistic activity, historical events are not possible; the experience gained from these events cannot be passed on without language. However, neither events nor experience are exhausted by their linguistic articulation. There are numerous extralinguistic factors that enter into every event, and there are levels of experience which escape linguistic ascertainment. The majority of extralinguistic conditions for all occurrences (natural and material givens, institutions, and modes of conduct) remain dependent upon linguistic communication for their effectiveness. They are not, however, assimilated by it. The prelinguistic structure of action and the linguistic communication by means of which events take place run into each other without ever coinciding.[36]

We can go further and acknowledge that the recollection of being comes with the

46

body.[37] Dallmayr suggests that we need a notion of community that recognizes the prior intersubjectivity of social life, and so far exceeds respect based on concepts of pluralism. This rests on a concept of the self and the individual based on an ontological "intimate intertwining" of man and nature, self and other. We are all in that case living in a state of knowing about the deep nature of the world but have 'forgotten' our knowing. We therefore have to become involved in recollection, but not rationalist recollection; instead it is

> . . . a probing of opacity or as an effort to decipher the signals of a precognitive or prereflective practice – a practice which is not synonymous with individual or collective designs which seem less akin to reason than to imagination (or to the poetic wisdom discussed by Vico).[38]

This landscape is available *in the flesh* quite unlike the landscape of memory in Dali's imagery (*The Persistence of Memory* of 1931) which is untouchable, or kept at a distance by the eyes. We need a remembrance memory which can handle the notion of language as of the world not as another part of the world. Memory then is a metaphor of the physical location (and language is physical and analogic first) in which experience is 'written', and I don't have any choice about what comes to me on the network. The notion of 'choice' may be retained in two senses; first about the limits of what a person can decode of the whole (the prelinguistic and the linguistic – the world and the word) through the language available; and second in the sense that whatever language is available it always injects the possibility of negation (different from refusal), and so I may start to choose, without any suggestion of right or wrong, what and how to read. This is where the view of language as carrying experiences as if in a container is exposed. The relation I have suggested is if anything the reverse. Language *is* a part of the world, and does not refer in an arbitrary fashion. However we are reluctant to follow the specificity of its referrals because we want to know them ahead of time. This desire to outwit language loosens the hold that language gives us on the world as an *historical* world. It is important to stress that this specificity is not the total knowing that a rationalist version of understanding in language offers. Instead it opens up an unending chain of specificities whose availability depends on not formulating the meaning in advance.

> It is precisely because language is something other than a semiotic system, because the referral in language is virtually total, that it needs no more than a single point of contact with the world in order to be enmeshed in the generalized and non-chaotic transgression which brings it into being, and thus to be able to speak the world . . . each language is a total cross-section of the world.[39]

I am therefore rejecting a notion of memory, language and understanding which gives priority to picking and choosing. It makes sense to me to retain picking and choosing as the social structure in space and time closing off parts of the analog continuous and timeless world, making a selection appropriate to one dimension of time and space but not empowered to limit my horizon and turn boundaries, which are necessary to apprehending the amorphous, into barriers. The metaphor of the missing or erased tapes is helpful but should not be pressed too far, since it suggests the mistaken notion of the brain as a super computing device interfaced (!) with other forms of information appropriately translated. Even the most elaborate version of the computing device imaginable suffers from the limitation of an inbuilt gap between its digitalized functions and the capacity to read and give meaning. Bodily creatures like us do not suffer from that limitation, though our truncated account of language and knowing all but paint us into that corner.

The crucial thing to follow from this is that the accessibility of the analog continuum of world and word is not confined to people who live in a particular location in space and time. The tie-up is not of that order. While this is not an entirely novel notion then predisposition of analytical thought constantly gets things back to front and screens out the richness of people's experience of space and time in cultural networks.

> In reality, every mutable thing has within itself the measure of its time; this persists even in the absence of any other; no two worldly things have the same measure of time . . . There are therefore . . . at any one time in the Universe innumerably many times.[40]

This suggests that access to the richness of history is not confined to those who have been located for a long time in one place and might claim in ways to have exclusive ownership of a tradition. I suspect that anyone who comes to live in a place can get access to the local *and* the extended history if they so wish, in spite of the suspicion expressed of those who would cease to be 'strangers'. Where I now live this suspicion is expressed in the word 'runners' to describe newcomers of up to 20 or more years residence. The crucial bit may be the willingness of a newcomer to penetrate and share a culture by testing the local boundaries and their determination to keep all but those born there. I can think of an English friend whose view of language and relations made it possible for him to listen and participate to the point of challenging local exclusiveness.[41] Over fifteen years of living in Ireland it was as if the weave between language and the world took on another pattern without losing the old – indeed he saw the old one as never before. The competence at patterning and inquiry originally sustained by his English locale was regenerated through engagement with the local cultural material. I do not of course imply that he became 'Irish', or 'went native' as the saying used to have it. I am suggesting something much more difficult, a willingness to let his language and his experience of historical time be constantly recreated through local social (and political) actions rather than be shaped from

48

what was affirmatively past and expressively present, his English life. I would claim that he was involved with me in a new venture in which "memory recedes in face of remembrances",[42] historical reconstruction of who we *are* not who we think (even with the suport of sound scholarship) we *were*. In some basic sense those born (especially of those born) in a place and time are shaped in the flow and form of life but my suggestion is that this history as much as they can take is available to *all* in a direct experiential sense. It is resisting this that gives us headaches, as we refuse to see and hear what we are seeing and hearing in our contacts with living people every day.

The situation now for me as a 'Protestant' is that I have *to go through with* the experience of pain not as regret but as grief, and take responsibility for the bits for which I *might* take responsibility.[43]

*Creation — The Context of Reconciliation as Remembrance*
Finding this new language is something to be done with other people. Reconciliation is a fundamentally social and communal form of action. We must find at least one other person with whom to create the comforting (con-fortis) physical context, for the real work of remembrance is disconcerting, establishing boundaries and connections while also simultaneously setting things adrift, demanding a new totality, a new order of context in which the new-found and long-sought subject is in turmoil. This we locate in a compelling and embracing narrative of history. In this we are not concerned

> to secure presence and establish identity by overcoming absence and repressing difference.[44]

This brings both peace *and* disruption, unity *and* difference, as we cease treating each other as stereotypes, and look for differences as the basis of communality. The change of emphasis towards difference and time means that we know the futility of the nationalist and racist myth of rediscovering the past in the present. Instead we are nurtured in the work of reconciliation through

> the possibility . . . of seeing the present from the point of view of the past, from a moment when this present . . . was entirely contingent . . . not the reiterative unreality of reverie, which emptily rewrites history.[45]

The creation work is taking on ourselves again as the partial origin of our own history and becoming again the origin of possibilities,

> as having had a history which was history and not fatality.[46]

Our recalling is to be done together and I know of no re-calling that can be without grieving. From this will come much needed new images of reconciliation. In the Judaeo-Christian context reconciliation as remembrance is the creation work of God in time, our time, the analog of then and now, bonded in my and your words, the cosmic time of creation.

# NOTES

1. This issue is central to social and philosophical debate and is renewed constantly. I have found the following delightful to return to: Grene, Majorie (1966), *The Knower and The Known*, Faber, London. The most prolific writer and the focus of much Contemporary debate is Jürgen Habermas. A useful review is his (1984) *The Theory of Communicative Action*, Vol 1, Beacon, Boston. See on him McCarthy, Thomas (1978) *The Critical Theory of Jürgen Habermas*, Hutchinson, London.
2. Harris, Roy (1980), *The Language Makers*, Duckworth, London (1981), *The Language Myth*, Duckworth, London. Wilden, Anthony (1980) (2nd ed.) *System and Structure*, Tavistock, London. Baker, Gordon P & Hacker, PMS (1984) *Language, Sense and Nonsense*, Blackwell, Oxford.
3. Taylor, Mark C (1984) *Erring: A Postmodern A/theology*, University of Chicago Press, Chicago & London. p. 14.
4. Taylor, op. cit. p. 14.
5. Aspects of the influence of the Frankfurt Tradition are discussed elsewhere in this volume.
6. Giddens, Anthony (1984) *The Constitution of Society*, Polity, Cambridge, is a useful starting point.
7. Hughes, Robert (1980) *The Shock of the New*, B.B.C., London, provides a constantly provocative and elegant commentary on this whole question.
8. A salutary reminder of others' 'revolutionary' times is provided by Marguerite Yourcenar, *The Abyss* (1985) Black Swan, London.
9. Castoriadis, Cornelius (1984) *Crossroads in the Labyrinth*, Harvester, Brighton. Pg. 72.
10. The presistent struggle to grapple with question of postmodernism is well exemplified in journals like *Telos, Praxis International, New German Critique, Theory & Society*, as well as a host of journals in the field of literary criticism, such as *Critical Inquiry*.
11. The phrase is Richard Wolin's.
12. Hugo Ball, of the Zurich Dada connection, quoted in Hughes, R. op. cit. p. 63.
13. Bouwsma, William T (1981) Intellectual History in the 1980's: From History of Ideas to History of Meaning, *Journal of Interdisciplinary History*, XII, 2, 279-291.
14. Inglis, Fred (1985) *The Management of Ignorance*, Blackwell, Oxford.
15. I find the work of René Girard important in this respect, as in many others. See his (1976) *Deceit Desire and the Novel*, and (1977) *Violence and the Sacred*, both Johns Hopkins, Baltimore.
16. Bateson's work has been influential in many fields. (1973) *Steps to an Ecology of Mind*, Paladin, London. (1979) *Mind and Nature*, Wildwood, London. In this connection we should note Humberto Maturana and Heinz von Foerster.
17. See references in Note 1. Two other names should be added. Wittgenstein is in every part of the story now, and Gadamer is carrying on the work of a renewed hermeneutic tradition.
18. Autopoiesis – a 'greek' word: self-making, self-creating, self-organizing. Prigogine, Ilya (1980) *From Being to Becoming*, Freeman, with Stengers, I (1984) *Order out of Chaos*, N.Y. Bantam. Jantsch, Erich (1979) *The Self-Organizing Universe*, Pergamon, Oxford. Influential but with a somewhat different set of assumptions is Luhmann, Niklas (1979) *Trust and Power*, Wiley. In a general sense the impact of the 'new' physics is taking a long time to digest: see Bohm, David (1980) *Wholeness and The Implicate Order*, Routledge and Kegan Paul, London. The following quote is not untypical. As for its argument that is another matter. "The existence, the life, and the warp and weft of interrelationships subsist in the Spirit: 'In *him* we live and move and have our being' (Acts 17.20) But that means that the interrelations of the world cannot be traced back to any components, or universal foundations (or whatever name we give to 'elementary particles'). According to the mechanistic theory, things are primary, and their relations to one another are determined secondarily, through 'natural laws'. But in reality relationships are just as primal as the things themselves. 'Thing' and 'relation' are complementary modes of appearance, in the same way as particle and wave in the nuclear sector. For nothing in the world exists, lives and moves *of itself*.... So it is only the community of creation in the Spirit itself that can be called 'fundamental' . . . The patterns and the symmetries, the movements and the rhythms, the fields and the material conglomerations of cosmic energy all come into being out of the community, in the community, of the divine Spirit." p. 11. passim cf Moltmann, Jurgen (1985) *God in Creation*, SCM Press, London.
19. Glanville, Ranulph, is an excellent source on this. See for example his: What is memory, that it can

remember what is it? (1976) in Trappl, R et al. (Eds) *Recent Progress in Cybernetics & Systems Research,* Hemisphere Press, Washington DC.

20. One of the clearest expositions of the essence of Godel's work is to be found in: Piaget, Jean (1971) *Structuralism,* Routledge and Kegan Paul, London. Castoriadis, op. cit. is also very clear and offers interesting connections.
21. Benhabib, Seyla (1985) *Critique, Norm and Utopia,* Columbia, New York.
22. The phrase 'Gospel Hall' refers generally to those groups within Protestantism who see themselves as holding on to fundamentalist principles. Specifically it refers to the connection of Assemblies in Britain and Ireland known as The Brethren, sometimes Plymouth Brethren (but not the Exclusives).
23. Barr, James (1984) *Escaping from Fundamentalism,* SCM, London.
24. Identity is a notion much bandied about in conversation in Ireland. I would like us to drop it at least for a while, since it has been captured in my view by a positivist outlook.
25. Castoriadis, op. cit. Pgs. 124-126 passim.
26. Maurice Merleau-Ponty is usually associated with Phenomenology. Let that not put anyone off from approaching him. His best known work is *Phenomenology of Perception* (1962), Routledge and Kegan Paul, London.
27. Castoriadis, op cit. Pg. 127.
28. *The Visible and The Invisible* (1968) Northwestern, Evanston, Pg. 218.
29. Giddens, op. cit.
30. Nathalie Sarraute (1984) *Childhood,* Calder, London, is suggestive of what might be done.
31. Moltmann, op. cit.
32. Habermas, Jürgen (1972) *Knowledge and Human Interests,* Heinemann, London (Postscript, Pg. 353).
33. Witkin, Robert W (1974) *The Intelligence of Feeling,* Heinemann Educational Books, London, Pgs. 1-2 passim.
34. John Berger's phrase. *(Ways of Seeing* (1972), Penguin, London).
35. Wilden, Anthony op. cit. is major source on this. This astonishing book is in a sense all about the distinction between, and the need to recover the connection between, analogic and digital modes of communication.
36. Koselleck, Reinhart (1985) *Futures Past:* On the Semantics of Historical Time, MIT Press, Pg. 231.
37. See Levin, David Michael (1985) *The Body's Recollection of Being,* Routledge and Kegan Paul, London.
38. Dallmayr, Fred R (1981) *Twilight of Subjectivity, Univ. Massachusetts, Amherst., Pg. 251.*
39. *Castoriadis, op. cit. Pg. 129.*
40. *Herder, quoted in Koselleck, op cit. xxii.*
41. *Irish Literature is replete with material on this, as one would expect given our 'colonial' history. See: Somerville and Ross, Molly Keane etc. Wilden, A (1986) The Rules are no Game,* Routledge and Kegan Paul, London. The debate on Ethnicity in USA and Britain engages this question.
42. Walter Benjamin.
43. It is clear to me on reflection that I have to take responsibility for the 'total' parts. I had asked not to have to take on Cromwell, but a friend picked this up at once, and I am currently trying to understand what this is all about.
44. Taylor, op. cit. Pg.
45. Castoriadis, op. cit. Pg. 26.
46. Castoriadis, op. cit. Pg. 26 passim.

*As this volume was going to press we learned with great regret of the sudden and unexpected death of Dr. Joe Harris, who had in his teaching and concerns striven so hard to encourage the reconciliation of memories. The loss to the academic community in Ireland as a whole is immense. We extend to his family our deepest sympathies. (Editor).*

# Testing the depth of Catholic/Protestant enmity: The case of Thomas Leland's History of Ireland, 1773[1]

*Joseph Liechty*

When explaining some aspect of Catholic/Protestant conflict, many interpreters of Irish history, ranging from propagandists to professional historians, develop some variation on a deep-rooted theme: that the relationship between Catholic and Protestant communities is naturally and normally, or at least frequently, peaceful. According to Oliver McDonagh, from at least 1800 all Irish nationalism was characterised by 'blind assumptions that Ireland was one and indivisible politically, and that religion was a false divider of Irishmen, used as such by British governments intent on maintaining control of the island',[2] and these have remained as unifying creedal statements for followers of both Tone and O'Connell. But the theme is by no means the exclusive property of nationalism. In David Hume's eighteenth-century account of the Irish rebellion of 1641, he was willing to acknowledge 'the inveterate quarrels' to which Ireland was subject, but he believed that 'during a peace of near forty years' these had 'seemed, in a great measure, to be obliterated', so that on the eve of the rebellion the pacific effects of English policy seemed to have 'bestowed, at last, on that savage country, the face of a European settlement'.[3] In this assertion Hume did not innovate, he only granted the imprimatur of philosophical history to John Temple's history of the rebellion, the standard Protestant account. In a very different context, historian Desmond Bowen has employed his own variation on the peace theme at the heart of *The Protestant crusade in Ireland, 1800-1870*. By his telling, 'the radical divisions of the two peoples which marked Irish society after the 1820s had not been found' from 1800 to 1822, when 'religious peace existed generally'.[4] O'Connell, Tone, Hume, Temple, Bowen: they are men with little enough in common, yet each has found it useful to assert or assume the existence of peace between Catholics and Protestants.

The assumption of peace seems to be the enemy of sound history. It encourages highly selective versions of history, allowing nationalist propagandists to ignore the real concerns of real Protestants by creating more congenial fantasy Protestants, and allowing Protestant propagandists to ignore the justice of Catholic grievances and their own share of guilt. The assumption of peace is usually accompanied by far too simple accounts of why this peace does not exist at any particular moment. Thus Tone and O'Connell pinned all blame for sectarian tension on the British, Temple and Hume found in the perversity of Irish Catholicism the sole explanation for the rebellion of 1641, and Bowen argues tht religious conflict began 'abruptly in 1822 with a declaration of war' in a single sermon.[5] The tension between assumed peace and actual conflict tends to produce either outright self-contradiction, or, as the price of apparent consistency, huge gaps in the historical record. Conor Cruise O'Brien has demonstrated that when James Connolly's historical writings treat of Irish Protestantism they suffer both maladies, self-contradiction and selective silence, but perhaps the silence is most striking: Belfast and its obstreperous Protestants simply disappeared from Connolly's account of nineteenth-century Ireland.[6] Bowen's *Protestant crusade* is a prime example of self-contradiction. Bowen asserts that 'religious peace existed generally' between 1800 and 1822, and he provides a couple of pages of documentation. But throughout the book he either modifies or undermines his own thesis, admitting at one point, 'most Protestants, most of the time . . . were not only anxious, but actually fearful of a sudden storm directed against them.'[7] Yet despite his contradiction of his own thesis, Bowen closes by nostalgically regretting a lost 'state of religious and social peace'.[8]

Put simply, the assumption of peace, in all its variations, is at odds with good history because it is a matter of crying peace where there was no peace. The cause of sound scholarship would be far better served by an opposite point of departure – that the fundamental state of Catholic/Protestant relations was enmity, whether latent or manifest. Then historians are more likely to assess realistically the formidable task facing those historical movements that hoped to effect some kind of mutual accommodation, or even reconciliation. We are also more likely to appreciate the fundamental questions each community needed to answer for *itself* to allow even a *possibliity* of genuine accommodation. For instance, a study of eighteenth-century Protestantism exposes a set of entwined questions that included at least the following: Are Irish Catholics human? Or do they simply need to be civilised? Are their actions subject to rational explanation? Or is accounting for Catholic behaviour a subject for demonology? Can Irish Catholics change? Or, for example, does the nature of the 1641 rebellion forever fix the Protestant response to them? Should Protestants attempt to convert Catholics? If so, how? What is the role of coercion? Of education? Of evangelism? Do Protestants accept guilt for present or past treatment of Catholics? What does that guilt consist of? Is the Catholic Church authentically Christian? If not, can individual Catholics be Christians? These questions, and others like them, arose naturally for Protestants as a result of the internal logic of the Reformation, their view as settlers of the native population, and their feelings of vulnerability to the Catholic majority. No doubt this set of questions varies from one generation to another, new ones emerging and others disappearing, with some questions always present but periodically shifting in importance, or even meaning. Historians, then, need to ask: Which of these questions were being asked, and how were they being answered? Which were suppressed, or left unanswered? If a particular scheme seemed to promise accommodation but attempted to skirt these questions, how did it propose to do this, and what effect did it have? In fact Protestants have proposed very few sets of answers to these questions that could bring a genuine accommodation with Catholics even into hailing distance. Answers acceptable to Catholics were unacceptable to Protestants, and vice versa.

A history based on the assumption of peace will always be unlikely to raise these fundamental questions. However, the cause of sound history will not be served best by simply exchanging one set of inadequate assumptions for another. Historians will do far better to subject their working assumptions to the most rigorous scrutiny, a task which might well begin by paying some attention to what we mean by peace in various situations. Overuse has so drained the word 'peace' that it has become an empty vessel capable of being filled with the most incompatible meanings, ranging from a peace that means little more than a lull between battles to the peace of full and deep-rooted harmony. More fundamentally, historians must test the extent of peace and the depth of conflict in case study after case study. What follows is just one such effort. However, it perhaps bears a special significance, because both the historical circumstances and the personalities involved seemed to make possible an accommodation between Catholics and Protestants. That such hopes were disappointed suggests the depth of Catholic/Protestant enmity.

By the 1770s the fields of Irish history were long since ripe for harvest. In an as yet unpublished essay on eighteenth-century Irish historiography, Jacqueline Hill demonstrates that by mid-century significant points of convergence between three major interpretations of Irish history – patriot, liberal Catholic, and Gaelic enthusiast – seemed to make possible a synthetic general history of Ireland.[9] By the 1760s, however, the basic assertions of these three schools had drawn counter-claims,[10] and now 'everyone (or so it seemed) was waiting for the "philosophical" history of Ireland which would identify the *real* lessons of Irish history.'[11] The Anglo-Irish community, with its peculiar position as neither fully English or Irish, seemed best situated to produce the necessary historian, and in the 1760s the obvious man for the task was Thomas Leland, a fellow of Trinity College Dublin.

Leland's classical scholarship had made him the best known and most widely respected of Irish scholars.[12] Furthermore, he seemed to have the temperament and approach necessary to produce a philosophical history of so contentious a subject as Irish history.[13] Perhaps the most important of these personal qualities was his 'superiority to bigotry civil or religious', which found expression in friendships with men ranging from Quakers to Catholics.[14] Probably the closest of these friends was a Catholic, Charles O'Conor, the leading Irish antiquarian, a writer on behalf of Catholic rights, and a man of great liberality and integrity. Beginning with an academic correspondence, their relationship became a warm personal friendship, and Leland bent rules to grant O'Conor access to Trinity's rich collection of Irish manuscripts, invited O'Connor to spend a summer with him in his summer home in the Wicklows, and drew O'Conor into Dublin Protestant society to an unprecedented extent.[15] In the preface to his *History of Ireland*, Leland acknowledged a debt, 'above all, to the zealous friendship and assistance of Charles O'Conor'.[16] Indeed the story of their friendship is an essential part of the story of Leland's effort to write a philosophical history of Ireland.

By 1767 O'Conor was urging a mutual friend to encourage Leland to take up a history of modern Ireland. The literary gap was shameful and Leland the man to fill it, for he was 'a philosopher, as well as a Christian', who would not 'permit religious zeal to extinguish the lights of philosophy'. Should Leland hesitate, 'let him feel the reproach, that if we do not exhibit a *Hume* or a *Robertson* in our island, it will be his fault'.[17] O'Conor wrote to a Catholic friend that he had indirectly encouraged Leland to write a history of Ireland from Henry II to 1688, 'to us the most important of any' historical undertaking. 'It is a pity that a man who distinguished himself thro' Europe by writing the life of a monarch of a remote country and age, should not bestow part of his abilities to adorn (and what is better) instruct and reform his own country.'[18]

Others were encouraging Leland, also, and by 1769 he had clearly taken up the challenge.[19] His progress must have seemed most promising to O'Conor. Leland told O'Conor that such work must be written 'with a liberal indifference to all parties English & Irish, civil & religious', and he requested O'Conor's help with certain thorny problems.[20] Leland's scholarship promised much, for he was proving to be an eager examiner of primary sources.[21] The relationship between the two men steadily deepened, culminating in 1772 with Leland's inviting O'Conor to spend the summer with him, that they might 'eat, drink, walk, and ride' together.[22] Such close friendship could only have made it more difficult for Leland to disappoint O'Conor's hope that a philosophical history would promote 'reform' – that is, greater Catholic rights..

O'Conor must also have been pleased with Leland's developing interpretation of the sorest of points in Irish historiography, the rebellion of 1641. Each October 23, the anniversary of the Irish rebellion, brought many a cautionary sermon from Church of Ireland pulpits. But the most important of them was delivered in Christ Church cathedral, an event described by historian Walter Love as

> the traditional occasion of rejoicing in the protestant ascendancy and of memorializing the black treachery of catholic rebels; it was a yearly reminder of the supposedly incorrigible disloyalty of the Irish catholic population, and the sermon in Christ Church was always preached in a tone appropriate to the governors from Dublin Castle and all their fashionable train.[23]

A sample of Irish rebellion anniversary sermons suggests that Love did not exaggerate – their primary purpose was to burn ever more deeply into Protestant consciousness the conviction that Catholics could never be trusted.[24] But when

Leland delivered this sermon in 1770 he took a radically different approach.

In a sermon customarily used to flail Catholics, Leland concentrated on Protestant guilt. To be sure, he did not take the approach of some Catholic historians and simply stand Protestant accounts on their heads.[25] But he did make sure that Protestants accepted a full share of guilt for the savagery of 1641. Although disdainful of Catholic teaching – 'popish superstition',[26] he called it – he acknowledged that Catholics had just grievances. 'Let truth itself bear witness,' he said, 'how far the iniquities of our forefathers contributed to exasperate, to confirm, and to perpetuate' Catholic rancour. 'When the gradual progress of their arms had extended their power and possessions, were the old natives, a spirited and haughty race, conciliated by kindness, by equity, or by justice? Or were they treated, where they could be so treated, like beings of an inferior order?'[27] Such sins were not mere memories. 'If we should consider the condition of our poor, or the conduct of their superiors, the manner of common life, or the characters and pursuits of those more exalted, we might possibly find abundant matter for an odious parallel.'[28] This theme Leland developed at length before concluding that 'papal superstition' was the 'the great and leading cause of this day's calamity'.[29] Nonetheless, he urged his powerful audience to 'charitably hope that Popery, at this day, hath been softened by a kind of tacit reformation. While we cautiously guard against all possibility of danger, we may the less scruple to indulge such sentiments.'[30] He hoped that by examining 'the errours [sic] and iniquities of our forefathers', Protestants might, 'taught by their example, . . . reform our own conduct, and avert the return of God's judgments.'[31]

In 1772 O'Conor must have been further cheered by a historiographical essay Leland published. His performance showed him to be all that a philosophical historian should be: skeptical of exaggerated claims, capable of close and fine reasoning, disinterested, and free from provincialism. And best of all, Leland's judgments leaned, in a moderate way, toward the Irish interpretation of things.[32]

During the year and a half that Leland's *History* was kept in the printer's shop by various delays and illnesses, O'Conor and his close friend John Curry, another Catholic historian and activist, were perhaps less than fully philosophically serene as they waited to see the results. First Curry got from the printer's shop oral reports of Leland's content, which suggested that Leland had written a strongly Protestant account, and later he actually managed to obtain sheets of Leland's work as they came off the press. He was more and more upset. The worst blow was Leland's account of Islandmagee, a massacre of innocent Catholics by Scottish soldiers. In a projected historical work, Curry hoped to base his account of 1641 on an argument that Islandmagee was the first massacre of the rebellion, thus inciting the Catholic response. But now Leland maintained that it had been a slaughter of thirty families, not 3000 people as Curry argued in his *Historical memoirs,* and it had happened not in November, 1641, but in January, 1642, as a Protestant response to Catholic killings. Curry wrote furiously, 'is Temple, Borlase, or Hume as dangerous an enemy as your friend? – I am really sick.'[33]

In October 1772 O'Conor read the illicitly attained sheets for himself. He found Leland guilty of both prejudice and sloppy scholarship – Leland had resigned 'his literary merit, and all credit with impartial men'.[34] Finally published in June 1773, *The History of Ireland* was greeted by mixed popular and critical reactions, and so it has continued down to the present day.[35] What may be said with certainty is that Leland's *History* never sold well and that it never achieved anything like the reputation of Hume's work on England or Robertson's on Scotland. But why this was so is very far from clear.

To examine Leland's scholarship fully is a task well beyond the scope of this sketch. What we may reasonably ask is how Leland treated Irish Catholicism, why he chose this stance, and why it disappointed so many of his supporters. His detractors put forward four main explanations of what they viewed as Leland's failure to treat Irish Catholicism fairly, all of them advanced by O'Conor even before the book was published: Leland was a poor scholar, he was prejudiced against Catholics, he wanted to sell lots of books, and he hoped for a clerical preferment.[36] The last three charges fall within our boundaries, and each is difficult to accept. All of them require us to believe that Leland's contemporaries completely misjudged his character, for he had a high reputation for integrity and liberality – this is the man O'Conor had earlier described as 'a philosopher, as well as a Christian', a writer destined for 'a superior orb', where 'religious zeal' does not 'extinguish the lights of philosophy',[37] as 'one of those persons whose benevolence is too well rooted by nature, to be extirpated by education'.[38] The latter two accusations – of selling his scholarly soul in return for popularity and advancement in the church – require us to believe that Leland was not only a knave of the first order for acting with such base motives, but also a fool of equal standing, because he misjudged his audience so badly that he wrote a party history that appealed to no party.[39] Leland won neither popularity nor promotion.

A simpler and more fruitful line of inquiry is to work with Leland's self-understanding: he was a Protestant clergyman doing his best to write a history 'executed with a liberal indifference to all parties English & Irish, civil & religious'.[40] From this vantage point, Leland's failure to satisfy any party does not indicate personal inadequacy. Instead it exposes the wide gap between Protestant and Catholic views of Irish history, even as those views were expressed by men of Leland's and O'Conor's high character. Leland failed, at least in part, because he had a nearly impossible task.

In discussing Leland's stance towards Catholicism, we will be justified in focussing our attention where most of Leland's readers seem to have turned first: his account of the rebellion of 1641. A comparison with Hume's treatment of 1641 in his *History of England,* which has become the prestigious standard for English history and for philosophical history generally, will help to explain the scholarly context in which Leland wrote.

Leland was keenly aware of the precarious position occupied by an aspiring historian of Ireland. Explaining in his preface the failure of eighteenth-century Irish Protestants to produce a history of Ireland, Leland concluded that lingering 'prejudices and animosities' were principally to blame.

> Time, and reflection, and an increasing liberality of sentiment, may have sheathed the acrimony of contending parties; and those at a distance may look on their contentions with indifference: yet, even at this day, the historian of Irish affairs must be armed against censure only by an integrity which confines him to truth, and a literary courage which despises every charge but that of wilful or careless misrepresentation.[41]

The image of a sword of acrimony, sheathed but lying close at hand, must have seemed increasingly appropriate as he pondered the mixed responses to his work.

Throughout the *History* Leland was casually dismissive, even derisive, of Irish Catholicism. In the reformation period, Leland believed, any attachment to the Catholic church was based on ignorance – an ignorant clergy and an ignorant laity were 'in proportion to their ignorance, abjectly attached to the papal authority'.[42] Hume's attitude was much the same. Commenting on the reformation period, he said that for Irish Catholics, the 'ancient superstition, the practices and observances of their fathers, mingles and polluted with many wild opinions, still maintained an unshaken empire over them'.[43] A favourable assessment of Catholicism, especially Catholicism in Ireland, was not among the distinguishing characteristics of philosophical historians.

When it came time for Leland to account for 1641, he paused to issue an aside. It sounded very like his reflections in the preface and showed him to be fully aware of the delicacy of his task. 'It is difficult, if not impossible', he said, 'for a subject of Ireland to write of the transactions now to be explained, without offending some, or all of those discordant parties, who have been habituated to view them through the medium of their passions and prepossessions.' His general task he understood to be 'to form a general narrative upon the best information to be obtained, with an attention steadily confined to truth, without flattering the prejudices, or fearing the resentments of sects or parties'. Specifically, he must 'trace the causes and occasions of a rebellion, whose effects have been important and permanent; and do not cease to operate even at this day, after a lapse of one hundred and thirty years.'[44]

In his account of the rebellion's causes, Leland steadily developed two themes: the pernicious influence of Catholicism on the Irish, and the follies of English policy. His treatment of Catholicism was harsh and conventionally Protestant, but his judgment of English policy was of a different nature. Leland cited two particular examples of English mismanagement. The Old English had been treated badly, which created dangerous tensions and resentments; and plantation, however laudable its goals, had been handled poorly at every step of the way, thus augmenting Irish Catholic discontent.[45] Hume, on the other hand, acknowledged no English guilt. In his account, the rebellion seems to explode from nowhere. The seventeenth-century English plan for Ireland, said Hume, was 'by justice and peace to reconcile that turbulent people to the authority of laws, and, introducing art and industry among them, to cure them of that sloth and barbarism to which they had ever been subject'.[46] The method for achieving these selfless goals was plantation, which Hume believed had been highly effective.[47] On the eve of the rebellion 'the pacific plans, now come to greater maturity, . . . seemed to have operated with full success, and to have bestowed, at last, on that savage country, the face of a European settlement.'[48]

To describe the course of the rebellion, both Hume and Leland employed violent and dramatic language, and both saw Catholic doctrine and clergy as fomenting massacre. But here the similarity ends. To the extent that Hume acknowledged causes at all, he attributed all blame to the lethal combination of the Irish people and the Catholic religion, while Leland assigned guilt to both Irish Catholicism and English policies. Hume described the rebellion in Ulster as 'an universal massacre', while Leland chided settlers for forgetting that 'their suffering brethren had, in several instances, been rescued from destruction, and protected by the old natives'.[49] Hume described the Irish as inhuman, Leland saw them as ignorant. Hume depicted the settlers as entirely passive victims, while Leland criticised them for their 'violent and indiscriminate' response to the cruelties they had suffered, which 'transported them to the very brutal cruelty which had provoked their abhorrence'.[50] Perhaps most important of all, Hume memorialised the rebellion as 'an event memorable in the annals of human kind,' characterised by 'cruelty . . . the most barbarous, that ever, in any nation, was known or heard of' and 'worthy to be held in perpetual detestation and abhorrence.'[51] This was precisely the role that the rebellion had always played for Irish Protestants, and thus Leland's account is noteworthy for the absence of eternal verities.

Hume and Leland diverged even more in describing later stages of the rebellion. Hume paid little attention. He did note that Old English Catholics feigned loyalty to England and detestation of the rebellion, but this was merely a ploy to obtain arms. Then, dropping all pretense of loyalty, 'and, joining the old Irish', their Catholic compatriots, they 'rivalled them in every act of cruelty towards the English protestants'.[52] Leland's account was very different. He pointed out the impossible circumstances of those Catholics who wished to remain loyal. One example was the Earl of Clanricarde, who, despite his extensive efforts to keep the peace in his area, 'was a roman catholic, and therefore hated and suspected by the state. Every assistance was denied him, and every occasion seized to mortify and

59

disgust him.'[53] Searching for an explanation of English failure to quash the rebellion, Leland concluded that the chief governors simply did not want the rebellion to end too early – Irish fury must spend itself fully so that those in power would gain from new forfeitures of property.[54] He also condemned them for indiscriminate use of torture to 'supply the want of legal evidence', citing the abuse suffered by the aged and innocent Patrick Barnwall.[55] While Leland placed most of the blame for the immediate outbreak of the rebellion on Irish Catholics, he placed most of the responsibility for its continuation on the Irish administration.

Such was philosophical history as written by the best qualified member of the Anglo-Irish community. The two main Protestant interpretive stances toward the rebellion of 1641, which were often quite contradictory, might be called royalist and parliamentarian. Although Leland incorporated elements of both, his work was definitely within the royalist camp, which had always been more sympathetic to Catholic claims. Where he innovated was in his recognition that Catholics had been abused and provoked prior to 1641, a point almost entirely ignored or denied by both parliamentarians and royalists. The obvious source of this argument, although he did not acknowledge it in his notes, was John Curry's work on the Irish rebellion. The result was a more complex than usual account of Irish history, but it was also quite useless to all contemporary lines of interpretation.

The most bitterly disappointed readers were surely those liberal Catholics and their supporters who had the most inflated hopes. Philosophical history, O'Conor expected, would not merely tell the Irish story more honestly than before, it would 'reform us as much',[56] perhaps to the extent of eroding support for the penal laws.[57] Given the written opinions of Hume, the preeminent philosophical history seems rather naive. It seems even more naive, or at least desperately hopeful, when we examine the various forces acting on Leland.

An immediate and towering barrier to O'Conor's reforming expectations was Leland's understanding of his task as an historian. History is 'philosophy teaching by example', said Lord Bolingbroke,[58] and his maxim captured a central tenet of philosophical history. But in a perverse way, Ireland has long been an island filled with philosophical historians who are only too willing to read their philosophy into history and then learn from the resulting example. Leland rejected this aspect of philosophical history and settled on a narrower task – to narrate events and explain their causes as faithfully and impartially as possible. Reforming the nation was conspicuously absent from his conception, and throughout the *History* he consistently eschewed anything approaching policy prescriptions. Any education and example would only be explicit in his text.

Leland might have served O'Conor's reforming purposes by reversing the usual Protestant interpretation, thus implying that Protestant fears behind the penal laws were groundless. Again, an immediate barrier: Leland's reading of Irish history simply did not support the notion that the usual Protestant understanding could honestly be reversed. His contentious account of Islandmagee, for instance, was based on a careful reading of manuscript evidence, and is now the accepted version of modern scholarship. But even beyond this, taking this option would have been almost impossible for any Protestant, and indeed nothing was really pushing Leland in this direction.

Of course Leland's Protestant tradition was steeped in anti-Catholicism. For a Protestant he was unusually liberal in the extent of his personal contacts with Catholics and his apparent willingness to extend at least some civil rights to Catholics, but he shared his community's traditional contempt for much of Catholic doctrine, and for what they perceived as the domineering role of the Catholic clergy and the subservience and ignorance of the Catholic masses. None of Leland's many published sermons had an attack on Catholicism as its theme, and in fact he rarely mentioned Catholicism at all, which makes the tone of his few casual references all the more significant. As just one example, in a sermon on miracles Leland used the illustration of 'a man skilled in mechanicks [sic], acquainted with the magnet or the electrical fire, versed in the experiments and processes of the chemical art, [who] might in a crowd of savages, or perhaps in a congregation of ignorant Popish bigots, easily pass for something more than human.'[59] The reference to 'ignorant Popish bigots' was an utterly gratuitous aside, but in these and most similar instances one has the impression that Leland was not so much seeking to offend Catholics or attack Catholicism as he was simply drawing an image from the treasury of shared Protestant understanding.[60]

Prevailing trends of progressive thought did little more to promote a positive assessment of Catholicism. In the mid-eighteenth century, some degree of anti-Catholicism was a feature of virtually every major system of thought. Penal laws had the sanction of John Locke, the patron saint of English liberalism, and while more radical modes of enlightenment thought might regard all forms of religion as more or less equally suspect, in Protestant lands Catholicism was a more judicious target – hence Hume intended his criticism of Catholicism's role in the rebellion as an implicit criticism of all religious enthusiasm.[61] Ironically then, his account of 1641, if sprinkled with a few scripture references, could have passed for an Irish rebellion anniversary sermon, which neatly illustrates the unlikely convergence of traditional Protestant historiograhy and philosophical history. The enlightenment was never likely to give an Irish Protestant clergyman a positive view of Catholicism.

The one possible influence on Leland toward a more favourable assessment of Catholicism might have been his contact with liberal Catholics like O'Conor. But O'Conor and company, in their desire to advance the cause of Catholic rights, had conceded many points. They had accepted the idea that primitive Irish Christianity was free of Roman influence, they accepted a Protestant church establishment, they protested against their exclusion from civil rights on the grounds that this was 'popery', and they distanced themselves from the kind of liberal and crusading political ideas that Protestants found in the Catholic tradition and worried about in contemporary Catholics.[62] A man like O'Conor remained a staunch Catholic, but what he displayed most visibly for the Protestant world was what he had conceded, not what he retained. Leland's relationship with O'Conor probably helped him acknowledge the possibility, even the likelihood, of what he called a 'tacit reformation' in Irish Catholicism, and it may have helped him to see that seventeenth-century Irish Catholics had just grievances, some of which remained down to his own time. But it did not create in Leland an appreciation for Catholicism as such, especially not one that could be applied retroactively to Catholics of the Irish rebellion era.

Leland might have met O'Conor's reforming hopes in a second way, much more subtle but also more fundamental, by acknowledging that Protestant fears were founded on a more or less accurate reading of the past, but arguing that no eternal principles could be drawn from ancient events, no matter how horrible. In fact Leland seems to have favoured this approach. However, he developed it not in his *History* (that would have violated his brief as narrator) but in his Irish rebellion anniversary sermon of 1770. It was here that Leland did his historical philosophising, and given O'Conor's profound disappointment with Leland's *History*, it is ironic that Leland's applications of his historical viewpoint in the sermon included a condemnation of contemporary treatment of Catholics by Protestants and a strong implicit criticism of at least some of the penal laws. This he accomplished by a two-pronged approach. First, he humanised Catholics by depicting them as not only sinning but sinned against, and he desanctified Protestants by exposing them as not only sinned against but sinning. But the way he dealt with the meaning of the past was at least equally important. In an earlier historical essay, Leland had expressed astonishment that the Scots should think it 'a matter of the least importance to the honour and dignity of their nation at this day, whether they derived their blood from Irish emigrants, or the native savages of Caledonia'.[63] In his sermon, he applied something of the same historical approach to the much more recent and contentious subject of the rebellion. Hume spoke for the Irish Protestant tradition when he said the rebellion was 'an event memorable in the annals of human kind, and worthy to be held in perpetual detestation and abhorrence', and ironically, men like John Curry were locked into the same general view of the rebellion's significance – the extension of Catholic rights in the eighteenth century depended on exonerating Catholic participants in a seventeenth-century rebellion. Leland cut through this knot by acknowledging the possibility that 'Popery, at this day, hath been softened by a kind of tacit reformation'. In a tentative way he had broken free from the pervasive Irish inclination to draw immediate and direct political implications from the past, working instead with a view of history that acknowledged the possibility of genuine development and change. Leland indulged in liberal and potentially reforming reflections on Irish history, along the lines that O'Conor had hoped for, not in the *History of Ireland,* but in an Irish rebellion anniversary sermon preached in Christ Church cathedral.

Although Leland's *History* was sorely disappointing to liberal Catholics, it cannot be shouted too loudly that there was equally little in it for Protestants seeking support for the penal laws.[64] O'Conor and Curry were disappointed that Leland had not reversed Protestant understandings of 1641, but from a Protestant perspective he had failed equally to uphold them. Leland spread responsibility for the rebellion among Catholics and Protestants, which was of little use to someone looking to history for justification of the penal laws. For such purposes they needed an account like Temple's , or Hume's, in which Catholics were perfect savages and Protestants perfect innocents.

If Leland's *History of Ireland* disappointed just about everyone, including some close friends, the response to it must have been equally disappointing to him. Although he was at the height of his powers, Leland never wrote another scholarly work. In the autumn of 1773, he obtained his first parish ministry,[65] and it was that work to which he devoted most of his energies for the rest of his life. He died in August 1785, remembered as a man of high character, a fine classical scholar, a devoted pastor, and a competent historian who did not quite succeed in writing a philosophical history of Ireland.

Leland's 'failure' and O'Conor's disappointment raise the issue of what may reasonably be expected of historians. Modern understandings of the historian's primary task seem to have settled less with Hume and the philosophical historians than with Leland and his goal of narrating events as fully and faithfully as possible. While denying the possibility of absolutely objective, value-free history, historians generally seek to keep personal perspectives and values firmly under the control of scientific historical methods and disciplines. In the dialogue between historians and interpreters of history (and it is a dialogue that sometimes goes on within one head), the historian's function might almost be seen as making life difficult for the interpreter by insisting on a rich and complex account of history which stubbornly resists the imposition of too simple interpretive schemes. Historians provide the raw materials worked by interpreters, who may be philosophers, ethicists, theologians, or indeed anyone else who wishes to try a hand at understanding the meaning of history. If historians choose to confine themselves to faithful narration they are not to be despised, for they have performed their fundamental and indispensable task. However, if they take up interpretation as well, they are to be welcomed, because they will know more intimately than anyone else the contours of the historical landscape being surveyed.

In Leland's circumstances his apparent failure was less a sign of personal failing than of the well-nigh impossible task he had undertaken. If success meant writing a history of Ireland as widely acceptable in Ireland as Hume's history was in England, Leland was required to provide nothing less than an entirely new conceptual framework for interpreting Irish history, an intellectual revolution he was no more capable of generating than were his peers. In fact his interpretation probably went as far in a Catholic direction as could reasonably be expected of a mid-eighteenth-century Irish Protestant clergyman. He wrote a history that altered Protestant understandings not by negating or reversing them, but by adding elements of the Catholic understanding. The result was a strikingly different picture of the rebellion, and in a general way of the relationship between Catholics and Protestants. Catholics and Catholicism were, as usual, depicted as villains, but they were not inhuman, or demons, they were human beings whose actions could be rationally explained. And the charges of villainy were spread around, because one of his explanations for Irish Catholic behaviour was the provoking folly and injustice of English policy toward them. Leland's was an understanding of Irish history that knew very little of innocence. But even at full stretch his efforts failed to meet the hopes of his understandably disappointed friend and counterpart, Charles O'Conor, who from his Catholic standpoint had extended himself perhaps even farther than Leland had. If any two men could have bridged the gap between the Protestant and Catholic communities, they were Leland and O'Conor. Their failure is a powerful testimony to the depth of Catholic/Protestant enmity.

## NOTES

This paper was first published in *Archivium Hibernicum* and is used by permission.

1. Jacqueline Hill has offered many helpful comments, and I am especially grateful for permission to read a draft of her essay, "'There was an Englishman, an Irishman, and a Scotsman . . .'": perceptions of Irish history, 1690-1790', which has been a great help in understanding the historiographical context in which Leland wrote.
2. Oliver MacDonagh, *States of mind: a study of Anglo-Irish conflict, 1780-1980* (London, 1983), p. 23.
3. David Hume, *The history of England, from the invasion of Julius Caesar to the revolution of 1688* (first published, 6 vols, London, 1754-61; this edition, 8 vols, Dublin, 1780), vi, p. 430.
4. Desmond Bowen, *The Protestant crusade in Ireland, 1800-1870* (Dublin, 1978), p. x.
5. Ibid., p. xi.
6. Conor Cruise O'Brien, *States of Ireland* (London, 1972), pp. 89-98.
7. Bowen, *Protestant crusade,* 132. For documentation of his thesis see pp. 84-5; for modifications see pp. 48, 83, 96, 131, and 141.
8. Ibid., 310.
9. Hill, 'There was an Englishman', pp. 5-10.
10. Ibid., pp. 10-19.
11. Ibid., p. 19.
12. For an English assessment of Leland's classical work, see *The monthly review,* xlix (September 1773), p. 205.
13. For Leland's approach as a controversialist, see *The monthly review,* xxxi (August 1764), pp.118-30; xxxi (October 1764), pp. 305-07; and xxxii (March 1765), pp. 191-4, which describe his pamphlet

battle with Bishop Warburton. The reviewers recommended Leland's authoritative yet fair-minded and polite 'manner of writing . . . as a pattern for all the dealers in theological controversy' (March 1765, p. 194).

14. N. A., 'Life of the author', in Thomas Leland, *Sermons on various subjects* (3 vols, Dublin, 1788), i, p. xliv.

15. For an account of their relationship, see Walter D. Love, 'Charles O'Conor of Belanagare and Thomas Leland's "philosophical" history of Ireland', *Irish historical studies*, xiii, no. 49 (March 1962), pp. 1-25.

16. Thomas Leland, *The history of Ireland from the invasion of Henry II, with a preliminary discourse on the antient state of that kingdom* (3 vols, Dublin, 1773), i, p. v.

17. Charles O'Conor to George Faulkner, 15 September 1767 and 13 June 1767, in Catherine Coogan Ward and Robert E. Ward, editors, *The letters of Charles O'Conor of Belanagare* (2 vols, Ann Arbor, Michigan, 1980), i, pp. 226 and 215.

18. Charles O'Conor to Chevalier O'Gorman, 1 September 1767, in Ward and Ward, *Letters of Charles O'Conor*, i, p. 222.

19. Among those strongly encouraging Leland was his good friend Edmund Burke. See Edmund Burke to William Markham, ca. 9 November 1771, in *The correspondence of Edmund Burke* (10 vols, Cambridge, 1958-78), ii, p. 285.

20 Thomas Leland to Charles O'Conor, 5 January 1769, in Ms. B. I. 2., Royal Irish Academy (hereafter, RIA).

21. For Leland's use of sources, see four 1771 letters between Leland and Dr. Ducarel, librarian of Lambeth Library, in John Nichols, *Illustrations of the literary history of the eighteenth century* (8 vols, London, 1817-58), iii, pp. 547-9, and also, Love, 'Charles O'Conor and Thomas Leland', pp. 5-6. However, a later review of Leland's *History* did criticise him for inadequate use of primary sources ('Memoirs of the life and writings of Thomas Leland, D. D.', *Anthologia Hibernica*, i (March 1793), pp. 165-7).

22. Leland to O'Conor, 9 May 1772, in Ms. B. I. 2., RIA.

23. Love, 'Charles O'Conor and Thomas Leland', p. 8.

24. For representative samples, see Edward Wetenhall, *A sermon setting forth the duties of the Irish Protestants, arising from the Irish Rebellion, 1641, and the Irish tyranny, 1688, &c., preached before his Excellency, the Lord Lieutenant and the Lords spiritual and temporal, and divers of the commons, in Christ-Church, Dublin, Oct. 23, 1692* (Dublin, 1692); Edward Walkington, *A sermon preach'd in Christ-Church, Dublin, on Saturday the 23rd of October, 1703, being the anniversary thanksgiving for discovering the Irish Rebellion, which broke out in the year 1641* (Dublin, 1703); Ralph Lambert, *A sermon preach'd to the Protestants of Ireland now residing in London, at their anniversary meeting on October 23, 1708* (London, 1708); St. George Ashe, *A sermon preached to the Protestants of Ireland, now in London, at the Parish-Church of St. Clement Dane, October 23, 1712* (London, 1712); Edward Young, *A sermon preached in Christ-Church, Dublin; on Sunday, October 23, 1763, being the anniversary of the Irish rebellion: before his excellency Hugh, Earl of Northumberland, Lord Lieutenant General and General Governor of Ireland: and the Lords spiritual and temporal in Parliament assembled* (Dublin, 1763); and James Traill, *A sermon preached in Christ-Church, Dublin; before the right honourable the House of Lords: on Monday, the 23rd of October, 1769; being the anniversary of the discovery of the Irish rebellion* (Dublin, 1769). More than forty such sermons were published. Later specimens exhibited somewhat greater moderation than early ones, but all justified Love's description.

25. Jacqueline Hill finds that the Abbé James MacGeoghegan's *Histoire de l'Irlande* (3 vols, Paris, 1758-62) presents an account of Anglo-Irish relations that is a 'mirror-image' of David Hume's ('"There was an Englishman"', p. 18), and John Curry's work (*Historical memoirs of the Irish rebellion in the year 1641* (London, 1758), and *An historical and critical review of the civil wars in Ireland, from the reign of Queen Elizabeth, to the settlement under King William* (Dublin, 1775) often exhibits the same tendency.

26. Leland, 'On the anniversary of the Irish rebellion', *Sermons,* iii, p. 5.
27. Ibid., pp. 6-7.
28. Ibid., p. 19.
29. Leland, 'Irish rebellion', p. 11.
30. Ibid., p. 17.
31. Ibid., pp. 17-18.
32. Thomas Leland, *An examination of the arguments contained in a late introduction to the history of the antient Irish, and Scots* (London, 1772).
33. For their agonising wait, see Love, 'Charles O'Conor and Thomas Leland', pp. 10-15. The quotation is from Curry to O'Conor, 12 October 1772, in Ms. B. I. 2., RIA.
34. O'Conor to Curry, 31 October 1772, in Ward and Ward, *Letters of Charles O'Conor,* ii, p. 30.
35. For the immediate response, see *The monthly review,* xlix, p. 205, and 1, p. 56; Sylvester O'Halloran, *Ierne defended: or, a candid refutation of such passages in the Rev. Dr. Leland's and the Rev. Mr. Whitaker's works, as seem to affect the authenticity and validity of antient Irish history, in a letter to the Antiquarian Society* (Dublin, 1774); John Curry, *Occasional remarks on certain passages in Dr. Leland's History of Ireland, relative to the Irish rebellion in 1641* (London, 1773); John Wesley, journal entry for 5 July 1773, in *The works of the Rev. John Wesley* (14 vols, London, n. d.), iii, p. 501; and Love, 'Charles O'Conor and Thomas Leland', pp. 22-4. For critical opinion of the later eighteenth and nineteenth centuries, see Edmund Burke to Richard Burke, 20 March 1972, in Burke, *Correspondence,* vii, p. 104; N. a., 'Life of the author', in Leland, *Sermons,* i, p. xliv; James Wills, *Lives of illustrious and distinguished Irishmen* (6 vols, Dublin, Edinburgh, London, 1840-7), vi, p. 148; Charles Read, *The cabinet of Irish Literature* (4 vols, London, Glasgow, Edinburgh, Dublin, 1880), i, p. 306; 'Memoirs of the life and writings of Thomas Leland, D. D.', *Anthologia Hibernica,* (March 1793), pp. 165-7, which was reprinted as Dr. Thomas Leland *The European magazine, and London review,* xxxvi (August 1799), pp. 75-7; Francis Plowden, *A postliminious preface to the historical reviews of the state of Ireland,* 2nd ed. (Dublin, 1804), note on pp. 13-14; and Leland's entry in the *D. N. B.* For opposite reactions of modern scholars, see Walter Love, 'Edmund Burke and an Irish historical controversy', *History and ideas,* ii, no. 2 (1962), p. 182, where he calls Leland's *History of Ireland* 'another piece of anti-catholic propaganda', and Francis G. James's much more positive assessment in 'Historiography and the Irish constitutional revolution of 1782', *Eire-Ireland,* xviii, no. 4 (1983), pp. 10-12.
36. O'Conor to Curry, 31 October 1772, in Ward and Ward, *Letters of Charles O'Conor,* ii, pp. 29-30.
37. O'Conor to Faulkner, 15 September 1767, in Ward and Ward, *Letters of Charles O'Conor,* i, p. 226.
38. O'Conor to Curry, 12 February 1772, in Ward and Ward, *Letters of Charles O'Conor,* ii, p. 9.
39. In '"There was an Englishman"', p. 20, Jacqueline Hill identifies as a central feature of Leland's work 'his reluctance to draw instant conclusions which would align him with any of the contemporary models of Irish history'.
40. Leland to O'Conor, 5 January 1769, in Ms. B. I. 2., RIA.
41. Leland, *History of Ireland,* i, p. 2.
42. Ibid., ii, p. 160.
43. Hume, *History of Great Britain,* v, p. 393.
44. Leland, *History of Ireland,* iii, p. 86.
45. Ibid., pp. 88-9.
46. Hume, *History of Great Britain,* vi, p. 430.
47. Ibid.
48. Ibid.
49. Hume, *History of Great Britain,* vi, p. 437; Leland, *History of Ireland,* iii, p. 128.
50. Hume, *History of Great Britain,* vi, 437-8; Leland, *History of Ireland,* iii, p. 128.
51. Hume, *History of Great Britain,* vi, 437-8.

52.  Ibid., p. 443.
53.  Leland, *History of Ireland,* iii, p. 138.
54.  Ibid., p. 132.
55.  Ibid., p. 164.
56.  O'Conor to Faulkner, 13 June 1767, in Ward and Ward, *Letters of Charles O'Conor,* i, p. 214.
57.  Love, 'Charles O'Conor and Thomas Leland', p. 4.
58.  Henry St. John, Viscount Bolingbroke, *Letters on the study and use of history* (2 vols, London, 1752; reprint New York, 1970), i, p. 15, quoted in James, 'Historiography and 1782', p. 6.
59.  Leland, 'Proof of Christianity from miracles', *Sermons,* i, p. 83.
60.  For other examples, see Leland, *Sermons,* iii, pp. 5 and 49.
61.  Hill, '"There was an Englishman"', p. 14.
62.  Ibid., p. 8.
63.  Leland, *Examination,* p. iv.
64.  Even John Curry, in his *Occasional remarks,* acknowledged that several reviewers had found Leland dangerously pro-Catholic in his treatment of the rebellion.
65.  N. a., 'Life of the author', in Leland, *Sermons,* i, p. xlix.

# Reconciling the Histories Protestant and Catholic in Northern Ireland

*Frank Wright*

The theme of this paper is that reconciling the histories of Protestant and Catholic in Northern Ireland is the reconciling of two opposed national histories. It is therefore a work with few precedents, because by and large national communities that coexist on the same soil develop in rivalry and antagonism with each other. It is more common for them to eventually separate from each other than to become reconciled. Reconciling of histories is therefore not an academic exercise. It is the uncovering of stories that are only important when they are of service to some pre-existing reconciling purpose. In the first section I deal with the question of why reconciling moments of history are likely to look like tangents to a history of antagonism. In the second section I look at the place of British responsibilities. Any effort by Britain to create the long term foundations for intercommunal trust, such as I believe the Anglo-Irish Agreement might be, will be greeted with mistrust which must be recognized as a fact rooted in the historical experience of British power and not made the basis for repudiating responsibility.

In the third section I will try to elucidate the process whereby the antagonistic histories and histories of antagonism have rubbed away any reconciling edges. Any lasting peace in Ireland, or even moves toward such a thing, would depend upon both communities recognizing how they had been trapped in antagonism with each other.

As an introduction to this discussion, here are Unionist and Nationalist stereotype views of the Famine that I have drawn up impressionistically from discussions I have heard.

> The Famine didn't affect the North much. Protestants are hard working and they got along OK even if Catholics in some parts of Ireland didn't. Maybe England didn't do much, but then you couldn't have expected it when there was Famine in England and Scotland at the same time.

> There were grain ships leaving Ireland in the middle of the Famine. Emigration and even starvation suited British purposes very well. It is still going on today in the North, where Catholics are three times as likely to emigrate as Protestants. Otherwise there wouldn't be a Unionist majority here.

Neither of these summaries contains any totally indefensible statement, but they reflect antagonistic perceptions of the role of British power in Ireland. This historical selectivity is an unsurprising consequence of the history of national antagonism. Whatever is "remembered" has a fairly direct bearing on the things that preoccupy people today. Opposing communities do not need to speak different languages in order to be different nations. The Orthodox Serbs, Catholic Croats and Moslems of Bosnia all speak Serbo-Croat and are distinguished as separate national entities by their different religions. Just as Irish Catholics often speak of Ulster Protestants as "fellow Irishmen", so Serbs often spoke of Croats as "brother Slavs". These formulae could mean either brother (with implied separate national identity) or little brother (who had to be taught that he really was a 'slav' or an 'Irishman'). Both Croats and Ulster Protestants, in order to rebut claims that they are really only subdivisions of the 'other' nation, emphasise their religion as that which marks them out as different. National groups coexisting on the same soil tend to develop their nationality in rivalry with each other, and the features of their histories that are most important to them are therefore the things that have clearest bearing on that antagonism.[1]

At first sight this statement may not seem to be fair comment on Irish nationalism which emphasises the more avowedly non-sectarian strands of its own history. But because it sees Britain itself as the main enemy, it largely ignores Unionism itself. It takes notice of Unionism only ephemerally and then only at moments of heightened antagonism, making the point that it is somehow an artificial product of British or sectarian manipulation. Unionism is treated as a one-sided repudiation of the "non-sectarian" Irish nationalist tradition; and even if it is admitted that Catholic clerical strands of nationalism may have helped to encourage it, it is seen nonetheless as an unjustifiable anti-national deviation. The United Irish rebellion of 1798 demonstrates that Ulster Protestants are "really" Irish, and would (or will) become so again if only certain British entanglements are undone. While conversely unionist histories tend to emphasise religious divisions, they too can use "non-sectarianism" in the same way. Ignoring the experience of Northern Catholics, some stress the economic benefits of the link between the North and Britain, and see Catholic rejection of such liberal "non-sectarian" arguments for the union as proof of their irrationalism. "Non-sectarian" gambits can easily be used as a means of self-justification and to cut off any effort to empathize with the experience of the 'other'.

It is, however, possible to build up entirely reputable defences of either position without any serious distortion of historical fact. All that is required is that the standpoint of the observers reflect the direction from which threats of physical violence, humiliation and denigration are converging toward them. Both will focus upon moments of antagonism because these are also most significant to both positions. The relatedness of the histories of the two national communities depends upon this forced relationship between them. The more locked into rivalry they actually became the more the things which defined them were products of the rivalry itself. Rivalry uproots any legitimate authority and gradually proliferates actual dangers which end up being the source of identity. As this happens the space for neutrals or doubtful members of each bloc contracts. Eventually memories of any less malignant inter-communal relationships are either belittled (shown to have merely concealed things that would blossom into malignancy), hijacked (to show how one community displayed a trust not reciprocated by the other), or forgotten (because ultimately they had an "insignificant" effect on the present).

What then would count as a reconciling of histories? First, if it were possible for either community to inflict a lasting defeat on the other, the mere fact of successfully eradicating the risks of further violence would tend to enshrine the 'history' of the victor community. Apart from my dislike of this prospect, I am also sure it is impossible in this situation. So, putting this possibility aside, we are left with two communities trapped in an antagonism. It is inconceivable that anything like a peace, a reconciliation of histories or memories, could ever be generated that did not recognize the mutual threat relationship as a fact. If it is not recognized as a fact it will always re-emerge as a spiral of accusations. How are fact and accusation to be distinguished? It can only be by recognizing that 'we' and 'they' have been trapped so that we have become part of the threat to each other. As national rivalries escalated, the justifications of 'our' side made the 'trap' look like a righteous cause.

The obstacles standing in the way of reconciliation of histories might then be as follows. The most important is that reconciling moments of past history are intrinsically uninteresting unless they serve some current reconciling purpose that is there before them. Secondly, historians looking for such moments find their work incomplete unless they also explain why these moments had so little effect upon present day realities. To do their job properly they are obliged to tone down the significance of whatever they unearth to reflect its current "insignificance". Thirdly, if the substance of national antagonism is the impairing or breakdown of mutual trust, many of the countervailing tendencies in the past – innocent of this distrust – did not even seem important enough for contemporaries to record. Fourthly, once antagonism has crystallized, people who are condemned to live in it often soften it in ways that attract very little attention. It is therefore difficult to disentangle all the factors which contribute to make better moments of the past invisible, unimportant, insignificant, etc. But without the hope or faith that there will one day be a better future, searching through this supposedly 'insignificant' past is like searching a pile of old bricks for cornerstones that the builders of nations have rejected.

To illustrate the second problem as I experienced it. While I was writing about nineteenth century history of the North of Ireland, I often came across people who are now largely forgotten and was strongly tempted to create "if only" myths about

70

how they might have changed the shape of what actually happened, had certain "extraneous" things not occurred. This was a rivalry with reality. I did no service to those such as James McKnight, of whom more later, I was trying to turn into retrospective challengers notorious figures such as the Rev. Hugh Hanna. I was failing to grasp how far Hanna's significance arose from his proximity to violence. As René Girard shows in his analysis of Dionysis of the Bacchae, the most significant in a vortex of antagonism are those who can both threaten violence and control the threat simultaneously.[2] It is only thinking about the subject of this paper that helped me to see that I had beem imposing upon McKnight and others almost a retrospective guilt for lack of "achievement".

The third and fourth problems suggest a different kind of difficulty. Who is to judge what out of the virtually hidden things count as reconciling and why? Once we grasp the moral chaos generated by thinly veiled or blatant force fields, the chair of the impartial observer disappears. Uncertainty of motive is the rule rather than the exception (that may be true everywhere but it becomes glaringly so in a field of potential violence). It is possible that novelists are better able to penetrate these zones than any supposedly scientific researchers, because they do not experience the same pressures to secure an "impartial" standpoint or to make proposals about what ought to be done. William Faulkner in *Intruder in the Dust* – a story that looks more like a political statement about the American South than any of his other novels – leaves us in doubt about how far he himself is speaking through Gavin Stephens. Stephens says that the South (in 1948) is defying the North in order that it should free the Blacks in its own time; but Faulkner shows us that Stephens has blind spots about what it means to be Black and cannot empathize with Blacks.[3] Rebecca West in *Black Lamb and Grey Falcon* cites a Croatian's summary of the Serbo-Croat conflict

> Nothing here has any form. Movements that seem obvious to me when I am in Paris or London became inconceivable when I am in Zagreb. Nothing matters except the Croat-Serb situation. And that I own never seems to get any further.[4]

By resisting the temptation to second guess him, she leaves this despairing judgement to confront the reader directly.

A reconciling function of history may be to find episodes that demonstrate the difference between knowing national conflict is a malignancy and mistaking it for a righteous cause. Such history will not have any visible thread or continuity, but will look rather like a series of tangents intersecting the history of antagonism. It will be partial, subjectively chosen and disconnected. It will have to be prepared to announce the importance of the "insignificant", "unimportant", and "ineffective". But we need have no reason to be ashamed of any of this. Martin Noth wrote of Christ:

World history at the time took no notice of him. For one short moment his appearance stirred men's minds in Jerusalem; then it became an episode in past history and people had to concern themselves with what seemed like more important things.[5]

The short moment lasted while followers and opponents held the mistaken belief that he would attempt to "deliver now" (i.e. politically). It is only the miracle of the Resurrection that makes whatever else Christ did and said visible to us. So, when we engage in debate about the Resurrection, whether it was an intervention of a divine superpower or a fraud or whatever, our debating rivalry over these questions serves to obscure the miracle – that somehow Christ is visible, though he would otherwise rank among the "insignificant" and "ineffective". The effort to reconcile histories is both necessary and fragmented. Necessary in order that we can recover the simple truth that we are made different by experience and not by inherent qualities. Fragmented, because in the middle of a preoccupying antagonism we know that the proof of this is everywhere; but we can only grasp hold of little bits of it.

At this stage it is necessary to explain how I see reconciling possibilities in the North of Ireland and the part Britain has to play in them, because all such judgements is necessarily political. When it seems possible that nothing will work, then we must admit there is only a relative relationship between political judgements made from different standpoints. This is all the more true because national conflicts do not, by and large, end up with reconciliation of antagonists. More commonly they are concluded only by victories or mutual separation. For reasons I cannot go into at length here I am convinced that neither of these outcomes will generate a 'peace'. Victories would not be final and the intensified separation would not dispel the antagonism. I cannot comment on the sincerity of those who believe otherwise, except to say that I disagree. The conflict is corroding not just British authority but authority as such, and without authority all justifications for violence spread like a hydra. The only possible authority – one which can be seen to place all peoples in Northern Ireland in a symmetrical relationship toward State power – is something approaching a joint sovereignty of Britain and the Irish Republic. The danger with moving toward this arrangement is that if it fails, it will prove rather conclusively that the external guarantees of both communities cannot bring tranquility, and will in fact lead to a degeneration into renewed tensional separation as the only remaining means of letting violence burn itself out.

For present purposes what matters is that Protestants cannot be expected to comply with an arrangement in which State power's legitimacy rests ultimately upon a nationalist majority; and Catholics cannot be expected to comply with an arrangement in which State power's legitimacy rests ultimately on a Protestant majority. Neither community could in the long run contain the confrontational pressures within them if placed in these situations. That is what either side's history of the experience of antagonism shows. But for an arrangement, such as the Anglo-Irish agreement might be, to work it will become increasingly necessary for its basis to be explained and taken responsibility for. Part of our problem is that before witness to Christian unity can be meaningful, it is necessary to recognize that the "religious" communities are, for better or worse, national communities. The use of religious-political rationales for conflict will be encouraged if the real reasons for conflict are not spelled out. To separate Christianity from tribalism will not be possible if a superior attitude is taken toward the very real experiences that make 'tribalism' a quite normal response to the world as it seems to be.

The ongoing division between Protestants and Catholics in the North of Ireland has been shaped by the presence of Britain, from which the descendants of most of the Protestants came as settlers in the seventeenth century. Even if 'divide and rule' was once a conscious strategy, as the antagonism began to involve ever wider sections of the population, there was no means of ruling that did not regenerate division. Internal tranquility, whenever it prevailed, ceased to be peace and became more like a 'truce' of communal deterrence. British power might contain the worst manifestations of antagonism (though it equally might choose not to) but communal deterrence meant that the potential for antagonism endlessly recharged itself.

This is scarcely unique to Britain in Ireland. Its relationship to Ulster Protestants was not unlike that of the German Reich towards Germans in its Polish border lands (Posen/West Prussia), or of the Austrian Empire toward Germans in its Czech border lands (Bohemia/Moravia). Faced with simple choices between retaining support from Protestants or Catholics in the North (or from Germans or Czechs in Bohemia), the central states, however reluctantly, had to align themselves with their 'own' people.[6] The frontier defiance actions, such as the overthrow of the Badeni decrees in Bohemia (1897-1901), or the enforced modification of the Asquith Home Rule Bill to include partition (1912-1914), illustrated the limited flexibility of the central state in dealing with their frontier nationals. These defiance actions threatened to produce Imperial-Nationalist disturbance in the core areas of nations and to dislocate the functioning of the state apparatus; and if all other methods of breaking accommodative relationships between the central state and the 'other' nation in the frontier failed, defiance actions worked. Each defiance action that worked increased the alienation of the 'other'.

In the long run, the different paths of Ulster on the one hand and Posen/West Prussia or Bohemia on the other, depended on the outcome of the first world war. The doctrine of self determination applied in 1918-20 contained no means of resolving the problems of mixed nationality zones. No nation was prepared to have its own national minorities left under the rule of the nation it had developed in rivalry and antagonism with. And therefore all self determination claims were mutually contradictory. Austria and Germany lost Germanic areas to Poland and Czechoslovakia because the peace treaties were written by the victors. By contrast the British retained Northern Ireland and the maximum land mass that contained a workable Unionist majority. Had Britain lost the whole of Ireland, it seems likely that Ulster Protestants would have been made a *cause celebre* of British nationalism in the manner of the "lost" Germans. Despite the creation of a system of devolved government at Stormont, the distance that has developed between Britain and Ulster Unionism since 1920 probably owes more to the fact that Britain never 'lost' Northern Ireland than to the institutional arrangements themselves. If this judgement seems counterintuitive, consider who would have predicted British enthusiasm for the "fantastically loyal" Falkland Islands before the Argentinian invasion of 1982.

The distance of Britain from Unionism today certainly has some positive effects. It ensures that Britain makes more of an effort to behave neutrally between opposed blocs than it would if it treated the North of Ireland as a test or touchstone of British nationality. Its efforts to preserve positive British-Irish relations in spite of the conflict in Northern Ireland are probably Northern Ireland's best single asset. It is the absence of any comparable accommodation between Israel and Syria over Lebanon, and between Turkey and Greece over Cyprus that has made these places what they have become. But the desire to keep a distance from Unionism has also prevented Britain from taking full responsibility for reforming Northern Ireland for fear of being unable to shed that responsibility if the effort failed. For example, an effort might have been made to respond to the Civil Rights movement in 1968-69 by reconstructing the North within the UK between 1968-71 on the lines of the US reconstruction of the Southern States – both were then faced with civil rights demands rather than nationalist alienation. But the refusal to override or abolish Stormont before 1971, though keeping Northern Ireland at a convenient distance from British politics, meant that British power eventually got stuck again in its 'normal' posture of supporting Unionism against Nationalism. The effects of the 1971 internment on the legitimacy of British power have been lasting. Thus the posture of 'neutrality' has often been a screen to diminish responsibility for something which Britain is very much part of.

The volatile and inconsistent behaviour of British Governments toward internal antagonism provides Nationalists *and* Unionists with very good though opposed reasons – illustrated by popular histories – for distrusting British power. This is now simply a fact from which there is little chance of escape. The best service Britain could do for people in Ireland is to make it possible for the different national groups to recognize the validity of each other's mutual mistrust. Only when that is possible is it also possible to create trust. Unfortunately, the path to any such outcome involves taking actions which – in the immediate future at least – increase mistrust of British intentions. It means attempting to place both national groups in a symmetrical relation to state power in the North of Ireland. As that means institutionalizing the guarantor role of the Irish Republic on behalf of Northern Catholics, it also means that Britain must eventually be able to fulfil the same role in relation to Unionists, despite their present dislike of the British moves to institutionalize the Republic's role in the Anglo-Irish Agreement. Movement toward this goal will be difficult and will encourage distrust of British intentions, but we will undermine the process altogether if we respond to such distrust with moralizing statements about "bigoted and intolerant Irishmen". The way in which the Anglo-Irish Agreement is defended will also affect what it will mean in practice and whether it will ultimately work or not.

Ethnic frontier national conflicts, by destroying the sacred properties of the law and uprooting democratic principle, help to illustrate what nations actually are. People in the metropolis, for whom these things may seem unproblematic, are allowed to ignore the fact that nationalisms are not merely 'like' religions – they are religions. They are, as Girard shows all religions are, built upon the sacrifice or expulsion of scapegoats. In religions we are all united under the sign of a scapegoat, and in the case of nationalisms the scapegoats are non-nationals. The nation state looks like a rational entity while internal disturbers of the peace can be isolated (i.e. criminalized) and the vengeful aspect of the judicial system more or less concealed from view; and while the conduct of antagonistic relations with non-nationals is monopolized by the state. The relationship between transcendental or universalistic religions and nationalisms seems uncomplicated while the problem of vengeance is concealed from view. "Give unto Caesar that which is Caesar's" has a relatively straightforward application. In frontier zones where the law relates differently to one community than to the other and where democratic rules are mere procedures in a battle whose results are never accepted (i.e. all self determination claims are intrinsically in contradiction with each other because no one trusts the 'other' with power over minorities of our people) the religious claims of nationalism are much more clearly visible. The scapegoats of each national religion are immediately present and cannot be scapegoated, so violence against scapegoats is never expelled. Metropolitan fascisms are only a variation on this. In their case, national vigilantes carve out for themselves a 'right' to attack aliens and "traitors", often in fact using "lost" frontier people as their pretext for doing so (as Nazism with regard to the Polish frontier or Italian Fascism with regard to Fiume). In these situations the religious claims of nationality corrode the transcendental religions. Whereas in Ireland the nationalities are denominated by branches of Christianity and not by language, this danger is especially severe because the line between the transcendental (Christianity) and the national is so thin. It is somewhat easier for Catholicism to keep its distance from Irish nationalism, because it is not an article of Catholic faith that the political unity of Ireland is sacred. It is more difficult for Protestantism because, if Unionist self description of themselves as British is repudiated, Unionist self definition is forced back upon Protestantism. Unless Unionism is recognized as an assertion of Britishness, and not simply as a perverse distortion of Christianity, there is no prospect of freeing Protestant Christianity from worldly (nationality) religions. These claims to Britishness may create severe political difficulties. It is certainly politically impossible to uphold them in the way that the majority of Unionists presently want them upheld. But if we do more than point out that Christianity be subordinated to any particular national cause without ceasing to be Christianity, if we suggest that a nationality is "false" because what distinguishes its members happens to be their religion rather than their language, then we encourage people whose nationality has been defined by their religion to make that religion a tool of secular politics and help to drag the transcendental down into the world of the purely political.

Let us now turn to the dynamics of the internal antagonism of which British power is the pivot. René Girard in *Violence and the Sacred* argues that much of our inability to understand sacrifice stems from our inability to credit it with any real purpose.[7] He argues that its purpose is to contain the dangers of vengeance. In most metropolitan societies the supremacy of the judicial system has cancelled the risks of circles of vengeance so thoroughly that we imagine we are too rational, too advanced or whatever to need to consider the prospect. In ethnic frontier societies not only is no such cancellation possible but each outbreak tends to increase the risks of future outbreaks; the mechanisms that reduce the risks never abolish them. That is one reason why many people can be found in the North of Ireland who know histories of the conflicts in their own localities in great detail, stretching back a long way. To demonstrate this point it may help to speak of a period in Northern history which looks outwardly fairly tranquil between about 1837 and the 1870s.

In Southern Ulster during the 1790s the British state adopted the Orange Order, which had grown out of sectarian contest between Protestant and Catholic weavers, as an auxiliary to suppress the Catholic Defenders. After the Act of Union in 1801 the Orange Order continued to be tolerated or encouraged as a deterring force in these areas, until the 1830s when the Whig-O'Connellite administration extended the centralized magisterial and constabulary system into the North. During the Under-Secretaryship of Thomas Drummond (1836-39) something like normal law and order was imposed in the North. Although it ensured that some districts remained largely free of sectarian aggravation, in many areas it was rather a tranquilized form of communal deterrence than a peace.[8] Orange landlord-magistrates and priests kept restraint over their followers, knowing that so long as tranquility prevailed, the centralized law and order system could and probably would criminalize those who struck first blows. Unless secular power can be relied upon to criminalize (i.e. isolate) any act of violence, it is likely to find itself intervening against acts which are already part of a circle that has generated reasons for itself, such as "reprisal", "deterrence action", preemptive strike" and so on. It then becomes powerless to eradicate pretexts for violence, and must either accept that powerlessness as a fact or become tacitly or actually partisan in order to secure at least somebody's support and compliance.

Communal leaders seeking to preserve tranquility, had to ensure a sufficient degree of control over their own following to be sure that they could prevent any violence from emanating from their 'own' (except of course where they judged that after a confrontation they could expect the state to need compliance from their camp rather than the other). And that meant showing enough sympathy with the "provoked" amongst their own people to keep influence over them. The success of the Drummond system, therefore, probably depended not so much upon creating a *tabula rasa* of sectarian dangers but rather on providing a framework within which local leaderships could successfully accommodate each other and restrain their followers. Obviously such leadership positions could be used for either tranquilizing or for confrontationalist purposes, but the serious danger was (and is) that it is impossible to be absolutely clear what intentions lie behind these kinds of leaderships. We cannot for example be sure, when an Orange leader preaches "readiness" against "Catholic power" and charity toward Catholic neighbours, whether the first injunction is intended to prevent actual aggression (and therefore restraining) or whether it makes nonsense of the second injunction. Until the 1870s, the build-up of Catholic society in some areas of the North (Schools, Churches, etc.) depended in the last analysis upon the protection of the centralized law and order system. Law and order authority in Dublin Castle was responsive to pan-Catholic pressures at Westminster. It was therefore possible for Catholic clergy to reinforce moral arguments for Catholic restraint with strong arguments from expedience. Confrontationalism could jeopardise any recourse to the law. When a plainly reciprocal aggravation ended up in local courts, advantage would fall to Orangemen.

In the 1860s Fenianism appeared in the South of Ireland, challenging both British power and Catholic clerical accommodation with it. In the North, Fenianism itself had very limited support partly because it was a manifestly unrealistic political strategy, but there was nonetheless sympathy for Fenian prisoners. The revival of Orange marches as a counterblast to Fenianism made it increasingly difficult for Northern priests to prevent Catholics from engaging in confrontationalism with Orangeism. And between 1867 and 1872 the Drummond system broke down.

The decision of the British Government to permit marches (after 1872) because it could not prevent Orange marches is an early instance of a successful defiance action. As centralized control over law and order receded, a greater initiative fell to the local magistrates. Orange magistrates who took the leadership of the Order were acting as a balancing wheel between Orangeism and British power. Toward British power the tolerance of Orange processions was represented as their price for keeping control of Orangeism; as magistrates they used their powers to both legitimize and restrain ritual displays of deterrence toward Catholics. Their leadership functions depended upon arbitrating the relationships between Orangeism and British power, representing both to each other.

Most of the nineteenth century history of the North of Ireland is "unimportant" from the standpoint of the present day. What is very well known is that in the 1880s politics and religion seemed to become one, and this was reinforced when the Home Rule question polarised Unionists and Nationalists against each other. Before then it may have been incipiently so, but enough energy was being put into preventing this from happening to see why it did so. When forced to choose, many people did so *reluctantly*. In 1840 when O'Connell attempted to secure the Repeal of the Act of Union, his reception in Belfast showed just how little Protestant support and how much strong opposition there would be to an Ireland ruled by the kind of forces he mobilized. But as I shall outline in a moment his campaign subsided in 1843 and anyway had limited effect in the North. In my description of the system of communal deterrence in the intervening years, I have stressed that the potential for polarization was never very deeply buried in some areas. But insofar as it was buried, it depended upon centralized law and order power acting as a moderating force upon potential conflict. At this time it was still possible publicly to call the threatened antagonism the malignancy it was, and to act in ways that visibly contradicted it. From these efforts, countervailing possibilities of mutual trust developed, even if their foundations look distinctly feeble from a present day perspective.

So long as Northern Catholics under clerical leadership relied upon central state power and largely eschewed reprisalism against Orange provocations, Northern Protestant liberals viewed Orangeism as the major local menace to tranquility and supported Catholic demands that it be restricted. But when confrontationalism became more reciprocal in the 1870s, not only did clerical restraint weaken but Protestant liberals who remained critical of Orangeism found themselves increasingly powerless. By slow degrees Orangeism ceased to be looked upon as provocation, and its ranks expanded as a defence against the very opponent it helped to provoke. Liberalism slid away from its outright opposition to Orangeism and toward approval of the more restraining forces within it. This process was already visible in the aftermath of the 1872 riots in Belfast and crystallised after the Home Rule crisis of 1886.

It would be absurd to attempt to make some kind of golden age out of the thirty years preceding 1886. From the point of view of post-1886 Nationalist, earlier clerical accommodation with British powers and Northern Protestant liberalism looked like weakness – i.e. a failure to match Orangeism. Indeed, not only nationalists but also some Protestant liberals who became prominent Unionists after 1886 began to rewrite the forgotten years as a kind of interlude in an ongoing battle. But the forgetting of these years was also a move toward abolishing the memory of everything that was not confrontation.

When people live in the shade of violence, they also live in fear of the worst things said and done in their name, because they know they are in danger of being held responsible for them by the 'other'. It becomes difficult to repudiate 'our' confrontationalists when the same people may be 'our' defender against whatever they provoke. The times past when confrontationalism was seen as a menace become almost embarrassing. History is gradually refashioned as 'them' and 'us', except when some telling point against 'them' can be made by suggesting otherwise. Potentially redeeming moments can be reinterpreted as illustrations of the 'other's' lack of good faith. Once they become debating points, they lose their reconciling possibilities. Benign intercommunal exchanges become inarticulate. Once there is a real history of confrontation and reciprocal violence between people, any intercommunal conversation about the things that divide may look like and become a challenge. Fear of giving offence becomes a barrier to any but symbolic or inarticulate displays of good will. Only antagonistic assertions are articulate and simple. We are represented towards each other by rival self righteousness, and any awareness that the other has reason to fear us is concealed from view. As such awareness can only grow into a coherent and articulate thing through open exchange of thought and feeling between 'us' and the 'other', it is in fact buried.

Let us therefore return to our introduction, and see what it is that has ceased to be "interesting" about the Famine and the events surrounding it. What is lost when we look at the Famine either as something which may have happened to Catholics but does not really concern Unionists, or as the beginning of a British Unionist strategy to thin down the Nationalist population in order better to control it.

Before the potato blight of 1845-50, rural crisis was developing in large areas of the North from which the domestic weaving industry was retreating. A fairly restricted and disproportionately Protestant area of the inner North, proximate to spinning factories, had become a well defined weaving centre.[9] The Famine destroyed crops (potato and oats), eradicating subsistence supplies of much of the rural population and undermining the livelihood of seasonal (migrant) harvest labour. But only in 1846-47 did food prices rise dramatically. In the inner North 1847 was *the* year of the Famine. While many areas with massive rural subdivision (especially those dependent on migrant harvest labour) were reduced to unmitigated destitution, weavers could (and had to) respond to high food prices or lower weaver incomes by intensifying their industry. Furthermore, after 1847 when the British Government placed the burdens of relief upon the Poor Law

Unions, dominant classes in localities with relatively limited distress could orchestrate ameliorative responses. Landlords still receiving rent, Poor Law Unions still receiving poor rate payments and Grand Juries still able to raise county rates had a more manageable task than their counterparts in areas with extraordinary relief requirements and a disappearing tax or rent base from which to meet them. It is therefore true that areas of the inner North experienced the Famine in a different way from outer Ulster.

In some of the worst afflicted areas, Poor Law Unions tried to refuse repayment of Government loans because they could not raise the local taxes, and charged the Government with evading responsibilities which they said were its own (an incipiently Nationalist approach to the crisis). If we look at the crisis in the North it might be tempting to suggest that this explains the different legacies of the Famine today. At one level it may do. When the Government in 1849 imposed a special rate ("Rate in Aid") on solvent Poor Law Unions to subsidise bankrupt ones, there were widespread protest meetngs in the inner North, at some of which people talked of taxing the Protestant North to subsidise the Popish South. Actual differences between the experience of different areas must explain how platform orators who spoke about "Northern prosperity" avoided being laughed at or thrown off their pedestals. But speeches about the Famine in the South being a divine punishment for Poperty (hence the exemption of the North) were rare, and became commoner decades later as a response to Nationalist claims that only Home Rule would remedy emigration. At one time things were much more muddled. There were Orangemen joining the incipiently 'Nationalist' protest against loan repayments in Cavan and Fermanagh, while priests and Protestant clergy co-operated with governmental schemes in other areas to raise voluntary subscriptions to secure matching Government grants. The short conclusion is that at the time the Famine was experienced as a disaster, and that even if its effects varied between different areas and (obviously) social classes within them, sectarian differences played a limited part in interpreting what was going on at the time, except insofar as they referred to actual visible differences. Later perspectives on the Famine of the kind I outlined at the beginning have lost interest in its shared aspects and the points of actual difference are implicitly magnified; for example the differential effects of the Famine may be part of the reason why state institutions (and landlords) were less discredited in the inner North than elsewhere; and contrasts between the industry of "Protestant" weavers and the total dehabilitation of populations elsewhere have a foundation in fact. As the repeal question in 1840 had already raised the question of power in Ireland in terms of 'them' and 'us', it would have been very surprising if some contemporary responses to the Famine had not been caught in the same grid. But what is illuminative is that highly visible political interventions were made in this period that cut right across the grid. And because they did so there are stories with reconciliatory implications to tell.

On the eve of the Famine O'Connell's repeal campaign collapsed and from within his ranks the Young Irelanders criticized him for the clericalism of his movement, for accommodating British power to secure clerical advantage in the educational sphere and public offices for repealers. For Catholics in the North, where the Whig reforms in education and law and order were a very real step toward equality and where public offices were very largely a Protestant preserve, these criticisms seem to have miscarried. And when the Young Irelanders came to Belfast in 1846 their meeting was disrupted by local Repealers. Francis Meagher attempted to tell the Protestants in his audience that they were right to oppose O'Connellite repeal because it was tainted with Catholic ascendancy, and to stress that Young Ireland was a non-sectarian alternative. *The Newsletter,* pleased with this vindication of their opposition to O'Connell, paid Meagher and Young Ireland the back-handed compliment of recognizing their honesty and sincerity, while using the occasion to demonstrate that nonetheless the real repeal movement was "essentially romanist". All the same, a group of Protestant Repealers organized a meeting at which R.D. Ireland spoke the prevailing sentiment.

> The real danger to Protestant toleration consisted in the tardy concession of privileges and rights to Ireland . . . as something to be taken from Protestants . . . when England should be driven to her own shores (and Protestants) left to an overbearing and exasperated multitude who have been taught to look upon them as their enemies.

It is very likely that the reason why considerable numbers of Protestants were prepared to identify themselves with Young Ireland was precisely because it did not enjoy the sympathy of the only force that might have made it something to reckon with, namely the O'Connellite Repeal organization. It was possible to speak preemptively in favour of Repeal as a possible non-sectarian compact because it was not being demanded by an "overbearing and exasperated multitude". The Whig Government had reasons of its own, connected with suppressing Chartism in Britain, for magnifying the threat posed by the Young Ireland movement's progeny, the Irish confederacy. It permitted Orangeism in 1848 to reorganise itself as a counterweight to this virtually non-existent threat, indicating in the process that the Drummond system of centralized law and order might be abandoned when it suited English convenience. But in the aftermath, petitions were signed by Protestants and Orangemen in favour of clemency for William Smith O'Brien, the titular head of the rebellion. And at an Orange meeting in Garvagh the main subject was not the rebellion but the need to oppose Government measures which it was thought would facilitate the ejection of tenants. In 1849-52 this tenant agitation blossomed into the League of the North and the South, involving Young Irelanders and the founders of the popular strand of Northern liberalism.[10] What they had in common was a view that the Famine was a common disaster, that emigration was a shared malignancy, that Government was acting as a tool of landlordism. Differences about religious questions and about Repeal were clearly pronounced, but in the course of co-operating, efforts were made to explain to their respective followings how the experience of Protestants and Catholics differed. Halting and limited their efforts may have been, but efforts they were.

It is very easy to argue away the importance of the Tenant League. It can be shown that if the chips were down on the question of Repeal of the Union it would have been split asunder. It can be shown that it was defeated in the North by sectarian questions, although in fact there were other factors operating which made it substantially more difficult for the Northern Protestant tenant to organize against landlordism than his Southern counterpart, not least that landlords' social role had not been discredited by the famine experience. Let it therefore be said straight away that for people today convinced of the uncomplicated righteousness of either Unionism or Nationalism, they will find nothing in the story of the Tenant League to shake their conviction. But for those who know they are trapped, they will find evidence of efforts made by such figures as James McKnight, editor of *The Banner of Ulster,* and Charles Gavan Duffy, the Young Ireland leader, to make a trans-sectarian class alliance work. this involved them in explaining to their own people what the world looked like to the other. In McKnight's case he had the task of persuading Northern Presbyterians that the infamous Ecclesiastical Titles bill – proposed by the Whigs and supported by all British political parties except the Peelites – was not a measure to defend Protestantism but an insult and offence to Catholics. He and Sharman Crawford, at a meeting in overwhelmingly Presbyterian Newtownards, spoke sympathetically of the plight of overwhelmingly Catholic South Armagh, where agrarian outrage broke out in 1851-52. While denouncing agrarian violence, they both denounced coercion acts, the "violence of property" and the powers of eviction or "extermination". When addressing Orangemen, McKnight made his views on processions quite plain by speaking of the "late lamented Thomas Drummond", reminding them that Drummond had pronounced the judgement "Property has its duties as well as its rights." Gavan Duffy, at great risk of discrediting himself amongst his own family and neighbours, went to a dinner in the hotel owned by the family of a particularly infamous Orangeman, Sam Gray, where a Tenant League Branch was inaugurated. Accepting that all of these things have left no visible mark on the history of antagonism, history can provide the stories which make sense to reconciling purpose. It must simply present the things which are now "insignificant", "unimportant", etc., without any shame or apology for doing so. The process that generates antagonised history works on all of us. We are all in different ways magnetized toward antagonism and rivalry. Reconciling history can only attempt to disintegrate the seeming coherence of the pattern by recalling the witness of those who, however "ineffectively", tried to do it.

If forgiveness is being open to a new relationship, concentrated attention on the events which have become central to the antagonistic histories is unlikely to provide possibilities for a new relationship. The mainline histories which demonstrate the reasons for antagonism, and which are remembered because identity depends on the direction from which danger and humiliation emanate, only help to the extent to which we learn *each other's* histories. This induces empathy with the other and checks the self justifying logic of our own. But this can only be a prelude to new relationships. Empathy with the other and a distance from self justification are *not* entirely new. What may be new – indeed what must be in a new order – is that these past precedents, feeble though they may have been, become interesting. Insofar as the national conflict in Ireland is between groups denominated by 'religious' identity, it is a question of searching for a history of ecumenism before the time when anyone ever thought of using that word.

There are things we cannot expect from such history. First, it will never prove the histories generated by antagonism "wrong". It will at most demonstrate how pessimistic judgements about the other, born of real experiences, turned into righteous causes. Secondly, what counts as attempting to create a new world will depend upon the type of world the antagonism is generating. Such history is therefore at a series of tangents to the antagonism and as story makes no sense without it. Thirdly, it only makes any cumulative sense because it is of service to reconciling purpose now. Otherwise from a purely academic point of view it will look like meandering. The only freedom we have in looking at our past is to choose a different angle of vision, to look in the past for the things which we believe have healing power in the present.

## NOTES

1. See Fred Singleton *A Short History of the Yugoslav Peoples* Cambridge, CUP 1985. Rebecca West *Black Lamb and Grey Falcon* London, Macmillam, 1982. Bruce Bigelow "Centralization and Decentralization in Inter Way Yugoslavia" in *South Eastern Europe* 1974, pp. 157-172.
2. René Girard *Violence and the Sacred* John Hopkins Univ. Baltimore 1977.
3. William Faulkner *Intruder in the Dust* Harmondsworth, Penguin 1978, esp. pp. 148-151, 207-209.
4. Rebecca West op. cit pp. 83-88.
5. Martin Noth, quoted in Werner Keller *The Bible as History* London, Hodder & Stoughton 1956, p. 357.
6. See Frank Wright *Northern Ireland: A Comparative Analysis* Dublin, Gill & Macmillan 1987, Chs. 1, 2, 4, 5.
7. René Girard *Violence and the Sacred* op. cit. pp. 13-25.
8. See Frank Wright op. cit. pp. 11-20; 44-45. See also my forthcoming *Origins of National Conflict in the Province of Ulster, 1848-1886,* Dublin, Gill & Macmillan 1989.
9 See the diagrams in Frank Wright *Northern Ireland* op. cit. p. VIII.
10. Charles Gavan Duffy *The Legend of North and South* Dublin 1886. See also *Irish Peasants — Violence and Political Unrest, 1780-1914* ed. Samuel Clark and James S. Donnelly, Jr., Madison 1983, esp. Paul Bew and Frank Wright Ch. 5 "The Agrarian Opposition in Ulster Politics" 1848-1887 (to be republished by Dublin, Gill & Macmillan).

# The Reconciling Power Of Forgiveness

Alan D. Falconer

How can I turn this wheel that turns my life
Create another hand to move this hand
Not moved by me, who am not the mover,
Nor, though I love and hate, the lover,
The hater? Loves and hates are thrust
Upon me by the acrimonious dead,
The buried thesis, long since rusted knife,
Revengeful dust.
. . . .
Then how do I stand?
How can I here remake what there made me
And makes and remakes me still?
Set a new mark? Circumvent history?

This poem, "The Wheel" by Edwin Muir, reflects a theme common among poets of his and of a previous generation.[1] W.B. Yeats in his poem "Vacillation" points to the way in which human beings are bound to their past, and, above all, are unable to break out of the cycle of guilt at their own sins of omission and commission.[2] This same sense of impotence, conveyed by a cyclic sense of history, is central also to the writings of W.H. Auden and T.S. Eliot.[3] A similar frustration and anomie is experienced by members of the different communities in Ireland in the face of what Séamus Heaney has called the "orphaned memories" of the different traditions The different communities live moments without context which will always stay with them.[4]

  This sense of impotence in the face of the past is matched by an equally powerful sense of impotence to fashion the future. In our contemporary societies in the light of the seemingly intractable problems of famine in Africa and of economic underdevelopment elsewhere, which are increasingly perceived as resulting from a lack of willpower by governments to tackle a problem which is capable of solution, a strong feeling of powerlessness has arisen amongst those working for a solution.[5] A similar sense of impotence with regard to the future is evident in the reactions to the nuclear question. Citizens of European countries especially are asking whether humankind must inevitably repeat the mistakes of previous generations. Edwin

Muir's poem "The Wheel" takes this sense of impotence up when it speaks of "Nothing can come of history but history".

While 'powerlessness' is a constant theme of Edwin Muir's poetry, the poet refuses to offer no more than a description of 'anomie' or 'Angst'.[6] As in his other poems, Muir suggests in "The Wheel" that the cycle, the impotence can be and has been broken. The poem ends:

> Unless a grace
> Come of itself to wrap our souls in peace
> Between the turning leaves of history and make
> Ourselves ourselves, winnow the grudging grain,
> And take
> From that which made us that which will make us again.

In his other poems, this grace is evidently the activity of God in Jesus Christ who frees humankind "to make us each for each/And in our spirit whole."[7] Power to break the cycle, the impotence, is proclaimed to be the work of Jesus Christ above all in making new, and in freeing humankind from the burden of the past and giving hope for the future.

This perception of the poet of the importance of Jesus Christ is echoed in the early writing of Hannah Arendt. She isolates two major elements of the human condition as imprisoning people, namely 'the predicament of irreversibility' and that of 'unpredictability.[8] In this context Arendt speaks of Jesus of Nazareth as the "discoverer of the role of forgiveness", a discovery which, she asserts, enables human beings to be freed from the predicament of irreversibility, from the constriction of past history and action, while the category of 'promise' frees human beings to be able to act in the future. For any disciple of Jesus of Nazareth these two categories of forgiveness and promise are essential, and are seen to belong to the story of Jesus. For Edwin Muir and Hannah Arendt, out of their analysis of the human condition as one of irreversibility and unpredictability emerges what might best be called "a proclamation" of the power of Christ, a power which is no less than 'the ability to change' a situation or relationship. Poet and anthropologist indicate the importance of power and the paradigm of power in Jesus of Nazareth. But Christians, while acknowledging this in theory, have often retreated into a cycle of inability.'

This contrast between theory and practice by Christians on this appropriation of the power of Jesus is stated succinctly by Monika Hellwig in a recent essay:

> We call Jesus Saviour of the world, and yet we constantly act on the assumption that the world as such (the world of human affairs, the 'real' world) cannot be saved but is doomed to perpetuate injustices and oppression, frustrating conditions of work, inauthentic and repressive interpersonal relations,

dishonesty in the conduct of political and economic affairs, ruthless selfishness on the part of sovereign nations, conflicting expectations and destructive values. In our liturgies and our hymns we hail Jesus as Prince of Peace, but in practice we seem to restrict the peace that we expect to find through him to peace of heart or peace of mind, while assuming that nations (including those that call themselves Christian) will continue to make war, to stockpile armaments and to kill for the national interest.[9]

Christians as well as other members of the human family have found themselves unable to embrace this power. Even at the level of reflection theologians have either been reluctant to speak about power at all, or have spoken of 'power' only in negative terms, seeing power as 'antithetical' to Christianity.

Among Protestant writers, there has been a tendency by some to equate the manifestation of power with sin, thereby suggesting that the Christian, if he is to be a follower of Christ, should renounce or eschew power.[10] Rather strikingly, to take some examples, in his major works, Emil Brunner does not treat the subject; neither does Otto Weber in his stimulating *Foundations of Dogmatics*.[11] Indeed as recently as the Melbourne meeting of the World Conference of Mission and Evangelism, a unit of the World Council of Churches, held in 1980, the Churches were defining their task as that of renouncing power and becoming powerless.[12] While there have been notable exceptions like Paul Tillich and Karl Rahner,[13] the tendency in theological reflection has largely been to suggest that power is antithetical to Christianity, or at best a reality that has to be tolerated.

This tendency amongst theologians reinforces a cyclic view of history and gives the impression that change for human beings is not an option. Paul Tillich has perceptively noted:

> The confusion of the concepts (power and force or compulsion) has prevented a meaningful doctrine of power.[14]

This confusion is perhaps understandable as a reaction to the concept of power adumbrated by some nineteenth century thinkers.

Nietzsche's answer to both the Enlightenment notion of progress and the sense of impotence of those who felt unable to be subjects of their own history was to stress the need for an intensified will to live, "even to the extent of an unconditional will to power and to supremacy."[15] Here power is seen to be a positive value as long as that power leads to "my" supremacy. There is no analysis of the nature or modes of power. All that is emphasised is the importance of power in helping 'me' to grow or develop.

Nietzsche's colleague and friend, Jacob Burckhardt, on reflecting on the results of the exercise of power in history, declared it evil:

> And power is evil in itself, no matter who exercises it. It has no permanency, but

is a lust, and for that very reason insatiable, hence it is in itself unhappy and must accordingly lead to unhappy results . . . Political authority takes it for granted that its primary task is to assert and increase itself, and power does not better man one whit.[16]

Here Burckhardt in his analysis of events in history is so struck by the fact that power has been used in such a way that men and women have been subjected to the will of people other than themselves. While a few people haver exercised power, the many have been powerless. Yet once again no real analysis of the concept of power is offered by Burckhardt. Paul Tillich's charge that theologians have confused power and coercion applies equally well to these two important nineteenth century thinkers.

However, the fundamental meaning of the concept of power is 'to have the ability'. The New Testament word for power (dunamis) means "to be able", "to have the possibility to do", implying both capacity to do good and to do harm. Indeed the application of the term "concept", to "power" is misleading. Power is a word for actualization, as Paul Tillich noted:

Power is real only in its actualization, in the encounter with other bearers of power and in the ever changing balance of power which is the result of these encounters.[17]

Power is the capacity to initiate the new in relationship. Power can be creative, rather than destructive. Theologically, therefore, it is not adequate to speak of the renunciation of power, or of powerlessness. A closer examination of the uses of power is needed. The New York psychotherapist Rollo May in his book *Power and Innocence* offers precisely this analysis.

*Modes of Exercise of Power*
An essential facet of a human being's nature is that he or she has the possibility to grow and develop – physically, mentally, and spiritually.[18] Human beings continually come to a knowledge of themselves. There is no point at which it is possible for anyone to give a comprehensive and final answer to the question, 'Who am I?' The individual is continually coming to self-knowledge through his or her contact with other persons. To be able to make his own self-affirmation in relation to others, however, requires strength or what Paul Tillich called 'the courage to be'.[19] This self-assertion is made in the context of the self-affirmation of others; it is in human relationships that we come to some sense of our own significance. Rollo May in his work *Power and Innocence* relates this idea of self-significance to the exercise of power. These are so intertwined that he writes:

A great deal of human life can be seen as the conflict between power on the one side (i.e. effective ways of influencing others, achieving in interpersonal relations the sense of the significance of one's self) and powerlessness on the other.[20]

May goes on to point five levels of power present as potentialities in every human being's life.[21] (i) the power to be — the fact that an infant's actions elicit responses; (ii) self-affirmation; (iii) self-assertion — the assertion of our self-affirmation in situations of resistance; (iv) aggression this arises when self-affirmation is blocked and manifests itself as the taking of someone else's territory for oneself; and (v) violence — when aggression is ineffective. It is important to note that all these features which are inherent in each of us if we are to come to self-significance are in fact terms of response to relationships with others. Thus self-affirmation is seen within the context of interpersonal relationships. The last three of May's categories, however, are all responses to a situation of threat — i.e. to a situation where the individual sees or senses that power is being exercised against him or her so that they cannot affirm their own being.

Rollo May continues his analysis by going on to point to those uses of power which, when used by others, can either stifle or aid the individual in the attempt to affirm the sense of self-worth. First, those manifestations of the exercise of power which stifle the sense of significance in other human beings and which, if they are constantly exercised, can elicit the response of aggression or violence. Here May stresses three different modes of the exercise of power equivalent to what Erich Fromm termed 'domination power',[22] viz. exploitative, manipulative or competitive modes. By the use of any or all of these, human beings in their desire to assert their own self-significance, and those of their values, opinions, life-styles and feelings, do so in such a way that the other person in the encounter is diminished and demeaned. The other has to do what I want him or her to do, and to ensure this I will manipulate a situation so that he or she can only act in a way which accords with my needs. It is very important to emphasize that it does not in fact make a lot of difference whether this sense of being made to feel less than human is in fact based on a true perception of the situation or not. The important point is that someone feels that they are being made to feel less than human, i.e. that they are being denied the opportunity to grow and develop in the way which they perceive to be essential. If they feel that power is being used against them from the same source continually then they experience fear or anxiety in relation to that source, whether it be an individual, group, bureaucracy or other states. Power, then, can be used to demean other human beings. Power can be used in a destructive way. This form of the encounter between human beings, individually or in groups, might be described as 'destructive conflict'.

But power can also be used in a creative or constructive way. Rollo May differentiates two different modes of this positive exercise of power, equivalent to what Erich Fromm termed 'potent power',[23] viz. nutrient and integrative power. Nutrient power, May suggests, is power *for* the other person: power exercised on behalf of another, e.g. a normal parent's care for his or her children. Integrative power is power *with* the other person, i.e. standing alongside the other, helping him, her or them to assert their own sense of self-significance.[24]

Although the above analysis has been conducted largely in terms of the needs of the individual and of the way power may be exercised in relation to individuals, Rollo May emphasises that this analysis is applicable also to what might be termed 'corporate consciousness'. A group, society, state or region may feel that power is consciously being exercised against them, whether or not it is in fact. If this feeling persists, and if the source of the power loss is the same, then fear and anxiety emerge, and a variety of aggressive or violent responses become likely towards the source of the fear. But equally important is the fact that power can be used in such a way that groups, societies, states, or regions can be helped 'to be'.

That analysis of the different modes of the exercise of power makes it difficult to adopt a rather too facile stance which points to the renunciation of power. All of us as individuals, groups and societies do exercise power. The question posed by that fact is rather, what mode of the exercise of power is to be employed? While all of us in fact exercise power in a destructive way and also in a creative way, how are we to determine a coherent way of acting?[25] Undoubtedly for some the principle of coherence will be 'self interest,' as stressed in the Brandt Report on economic development even if that principle is to be modified to "enlightened self interest".[26] For the Christian churches, however, the principle of coherence must be related to the activity of God. What might theology have to say on reflecting on the analysis of power which we have undertaken?

### Theological Reflection on the Exercise of Power

Power is capable of being exercised in both positive and negative ways. The portrayal of God's activity, especially in the Bible, tends towards an emphasis on the positive modes of exercise of power.

In creation, God acts in such a way that the creatures can respond freely to each other and to Him. In a phrase made prominent by John Macquarrie, what is most typical of God is his "letting-be", his conferring of being, his self-giving to the beings. This letting-be is both his creativity and his love.[27] Macquarrie goes on to emphasise that this "letting-be" is not to be understood as a standing off from someone or something, but is a positive work of 'enabling to be'. He suggests that we are to understand "letting" as "empowering" and "be" as "enjoying the maximal range of being that is open to the particular being concerned."[28] 'Letting be' therefore would be 'empowering for life in its fullness.'

This 'letting be' which is a positive exercise of power is described by Geddes MacGregor, the American theologian, as sacrificial love. The divine power is:

> . . . the power of sacrificial love. God does not control his creatures; he graciously lets them be . . . Not only does God bring creatures into being to let them be; he creatively restores whatever seeks such restoration, so that the redeemed might indeed well be called a new creation, that is, a re-creation.[29]

While the activity of God as depicted throughout the Bible and Christian history may be characterized as a divine-human encounter in which God empowers human beings to be, such an activity is above all seen in Jesus Christ.

The Incarnation shows forth the being of God 'with us'. In emphasising the title 'Emmanuel' – God with us – in respect of Jesus, Matthew draws not only on an Isaiahnic expectation,[30] but also on an awareness of a God who travelled with the people confronting them through specific conflicts.[31] Through these conflicts He widened their horizons so that they, the people, may have a fuller relationship with God and other people. Through this divine-human encounter, the people of God were reminded of their Covenant with God in which God empowered them to be. Through this divine-human encounter, the people of God were brought under judgement for exercising power in a way which tried to coerce, exploit or manipulate others. The prophets, for example, charge the people with this precisely because it is destructive of relationships within and between communities, and does not reflect the way God has let them be, as is evident in the writings of Amos, Hosea, Ezekiel and Jeremiah, amongst others.

Above all, the Christian community saw this activity of God empowering people in Jesus Christ. The letter to the *Ephesians* is a thoughtful articulation of the way in which the Early Church saw that Christ had enabled diverse individuals and groups 'to be', drawing them into a positive relationship with each other and with God. This is portrayed in the development of the concept, Peace, throughout the Letter. The Ephesian letter is, however, no more than a reflection on the being of Jesus, as far as that can be discerned. In the Gospels, Jesus empowers human beings, – enabling them 'to be'. He frees people from their pasts so that they can enter positive relationships with each other, e.g. Zaccheus. To take another example, the people in general, because their history inhibited any relationship of positive worth with the Samaritans, are freed 'to be' when a Samaritan is placed as the example of who is being most faithful to God in the Parable of 'the Good Samaritan'. By his use of 'integrative' power – standing alongside people empowering them – helping them 'to be' – Jesus provoked conflict. His very conduct acted as a judgement on those who sought to enter relationships by trying to control, manipulate or coerce people in such a way that the other is destroyed. Because of the way Jesus exercised power he was deemed to be a threat, and was therefore ridiculed, arraigned and eventually crucified.[32]

In this activity of liberating and empowering, the forgiveness of sins was a crucial factor. It was above all though forgiveness that Jesus of Nazareth seems to have liberated men and women from the burden of their pasts. I do not suggest that the past becomes unimportant, but that the past is no longer a burden. I shall explore this further in a later section. In telling the story of Jesus of Nazareth, a central place is given by the Gospel writers to his activity in forgiving. From the very call of repentance by John the Baptist to the petition from the Cross, "Father, forgive them . . ." the forgiveness of sin appears as a leitmotif in the Gospel; to such an extent that, as we have noted, Hannah Arendt attributes the discovery of the role of forgiveness in the realm of human affairs to Jesus of Nazareth. It is through this forgiveness that Jesus stands alongside men and women empowering them to be. Forgiveness is an act of 'integrative power' enabling the other to be, enabling the other to take responsibility for himself or herself.

In exploring the relationship between forgiveness and the modes of power, it is instructive to note those exercises of power which Jesus of Nazareth seems to have rejected.

In his study *The Forgiveness of Sins,* the English novelist, poet and theological writer, Charles Williams, points to the importance of the temptations of Jesus as the renunciation of 'destructive' uses of power.[33] God can only be loved and glorified by free people. Manipulation, coercion and competition constrain people to act and think what another demands that they act and think. If Jesus rejects the destructive modes of the exercise of power, then he equally rejects the 'nutrient' mode of the exercise of power. Jesus does not seem to take decisions for others, nor to think on behalf of others.

The very style of Jesus' teaching in parables requires the listener to respond, to think the matter through and act accordingly. Such a style of teaching is, of course, conflictual, jolting the listener out of concern with self and the maintenance of the status quo. The healing activity of Jesus also aims at empowering people to take responsibility for their lives in such a way that they are not bound by the infirmities of their pasts. The exercise of 'integrative power' is above all characterised by Jesus' activity in forgiveness. Through the forgiveness of sin the other is freed from the burden of the past and is empowered to take responsibility for his or her own actions. Hannah Arendt has written perceptively of this:

> Only through this constant release from what they do can men (and women) remain free agents, only by constant willingness to change their minds and start again can they be trusted with so great a power as that to begin something new.[34]

This release which leads to freedom involves the subject embracing responsibility for past and future actions. The classic example of this in the Gospels is the story of Zaccheus who takes responsibility for his past by acts of restitution and who seems to embrace responsibility for his future thought and action, although this is in fact only implied by his encounter with Jesus. In this exercise of power Jesus enables Zaccheus to become a free agent. This forgiveness is called "a power, an energy" by Charles Williams.[35]

In exploring this understanding of the forgiveness of sin as an exercise of integrative power it is important to expose the effect of sin. Sin basically denotes a broken relationship. By a hasty word, lack of consideration or sensitivity we harm other people, even people whom we like or love. Often we exercise power over people, manipulating them so that they will think or do what we want them to think or do. At times we give people no option but to act according to our needs and expectations rather than their own. Through this we do not take the other seriously. The effect of this is that neither of us is able to be ourselves, to be free. The effect of this sin is that we carry round a certan burden of guilt with us. Every time we meet the other, there is an awareness of the way we parted at the last encounter. We are not free to develop the relationship. Either we avoid the person because we remember how things were between us on a previous occasion. Or we feel free to develop the relationship only in the way it had been previously; thus we continue to try to manipulate. We are not free to let the relationship be one of mutuality.

This account of the effect of sin applies not only in the relationship between individuals, but also that between groups and also to relationship with God. The history of humankind's dealing with God as seen in Scripture and the history of the Church is riddled with the attempts by men, women and societies to manipulate God and tie God down to human caricatures and stereotypes. The history of the dealings of human communities with one another is no less destructive. Irish history throws up countless examples of the way in which one community tried to control the other communities by manipulation or coercion. Such an exercise of power was either condoned or at least not condemned by the respective Christian traditions. There was little 'empowering' in this spiral of alienation. Both the manipulator and the manipulated, the oppressor and the oppressed have become imprisoned by the ensuing relationship, and carry the respective pain with them.

The forgiveness of sin, which is quite undeserved and unexpected, enables relationships to be freed from the burden of the past and to grow in a more wholesome way. As Hannah Arendt notes:

> Forgiving, in other words, is the only reaction which does not merely re-act but acts anew and unexpectedly, unconditioned by the act which provoked it and therefore freeing from its consequences both the one who forgives and the one who is forgiven. [36]

Forgiveness, then, is an exercise of power itself, which counteracts the destructive modes of the exercise of power and releases people to act anew. Such an exercise of power on the part of Jesus reflects his being-with-others.

It is this quality of Jesus' being-with-us which I think theological tradition has tried to characterize in 'kenotic Christology'. While kenotic Christology tended to imply that God gave up his Godness or divinity to act with human beings so that they might be empowered, it seems rather that this kenosis is in fact descriptive of the very being of God. I take it that this is precisely what John MacQuarrie, Geddes MacGregor and Paul Tillich are affirming with their starting points in the understanding of 'being', in trying to understand the nature of God as 'He Who Lets Be.' This is also what Jürgen Moltmann with his starting point in the suffering of God is trying to affirm.[37] Kenotic Christology asserts that Jesus is He Who Lets us Be, empowering us so that we can enter relationships with each other and with God. Jesus acts with men and women in such a way that their response to him and others is free and in this activity of empowering others, he demonstrates his vulnerability. The life of Jesus is an affirmation of 'integrative power' – of being with men and women in the ambiguity of human life.

*Towards the 'Reconciliation of Memories'.*
The implications of the characterization of forgiveness as 'integrative power' are enormous. The activity of forgiveness involves the partners of a relationship. Nobody can seek forgiveness on behalf of another. Nor can forgiveness be sought out of self-interest, as that would be another attempt at manipulating the relationship. Roger Schutz, prior of the Taizé Community, has written:

> You can never forgive out of self-interest, to change the other person. That would be a miserable calculation which has nothing to do with the free gift of love. You can only forgive because of Christ.[38]

> The striking witness to the power of forgiveness which emerges so often from the pages of the diaries of so many Holocaust victims lies precisely in the fact that they enunciate forgiveness. No one can do it on their behalf. It is their relationships which have been fractured. They take responsibility for trying to create a new beginning.[39]

For those, then, who have perceived the unique importance of the forgiveness of sin offered by Jesus of Nazareth and who stand in the event of Jesus Christ, they themselves need to become a community of the forgiveness of sin, as a sign or sacrament of that activity of Jesus of Nazareth. There are serious questions, therefore, which need to be addressed to all the churches. Within our communities are we dominated by this integrative power of the forgiveness of sin? Do we continually make all things new? Do some in the church try to manipulate or control others? Why is it that so many people (women especially) are asking why it is in the church they they feel least free? In my own ecclesiastical tradition and quite contrary to the teaching of our Reformation father, John Calvin, we have no tradition of Confession, other than in prayers of confession.[40] Can any church tradition afford not to have an internal structure for the process of forgiveness?

The story of relations between Christian communities has been as subject to fracture and alienation as relations between human beings. The Christian communities carry the memory of the events of the various ruptures, from which they have developed their identities over and against the others. As Rowan

Williams in his stimulating book *Resurrection* observes, these memories are far from being congenial and painless since

> Memory is the memory of our responsibility for rejection and injury, for diminution of self and others.[41]

These memories of past injury and pain are carried with us, as they have formed our contemporary stances, postures and identities. They imprison us in relationships fashioned prior to our era, yet sustained and nourished in us by the appropriation of our heritage. Only forgiveness can break the cycle. But forgiveness involves the acceptances of responsibility for our actions as Christian communities in relation to each other, and for the fracture in our relationships which we perpetuate because of our memories.

The Presbyterian tradition, for example, adopted its system of church government largely because the system of episcopacy had become corrupted in the sixteenth century to a point where the church was unable to be a disciplined community empowering people.[42] The Reformers adopted this church polity as a direct consequence of the inability of the episcopal system to let the church be the church. The concern of the Reformers was to reform the church so that it could be a community of integrity. Their subsequent presbyteral polity was determined by those churches who operated an episcopal system but who had allowed it to become a system for manipulating the church to further the power of kings or political powers.

In the recent improved relations between Christian communities, the differing communities have sought reconciliation, and have asked forgiveness for the hurt and the pain of the events which have fractured relationships.[43] Yet a large number of moves towards reconciliation and unity have been dashed on the rocks of the irreconcilability of episcopal and presbyteral polities.[44] The churches, including the churches on this island, have become prisoners of their own pasts. There seems to be little possibility of the reconciliation of their memories.

Forgiveness, however, is about accepting responsibility for past actions. When episcopal Churches seek forgiveness for their past in creating a situation which led to the necessity for others to adopt a different polity, it is not enough for them to ask for forgiveness and then make as a condition for reconciliation that the others adopt the episcopal system as a *sine qua non* for that reconciliation.[45] The process of forgiveness involves the acceptance of our responsibility, the sharing of the pain of broken relationship and the preparedness to change so that both communities can be free to be. This does not mean that episcopal churches must become presbyterian in polity before reconciliation is possible. It does mean that the primary question for the reconciliation of those Christian traditions acknowledging and appropriating the past rupture is 'how best can the church be the church today?'. What structures are the most appropriate for the Christian community attempting to live the life-style of 'empowerment'? It may be that out of that question will emerge a polity of bishop-in-presbytery. However, other polities could easily arise out of such an examination. By seriously asking the question, however, of how the Church might best be structured today, both Episcopalians and Presbyterians are freed from the past and enabled to move towards reconciliation. Such a reconciliation of memories, then, involves the process of seeking forgiveness, accepting responsibility for the past actions of 'our' community which belong to the memory of both parties, and by appropriating the history of the other who has been shaped by 'our' past actions to learn from their experiences which are not shared with 'us'. Through this process of forgiveness both are empowered to be and to enter a new relationship which is able to embrace the memories of the hurt and alienation.

The resolution of the conflict and experiences of the different ecclesiastical polities is not the only example that might have been taken, though it has proved to be an important one in interchurch relations. Mark Santer, for example, in his essay on *The Reconciliation of Memories*[46] begins with the need to appropriate each other's martyrs. The analysis of the reconciliation of polities, however, has enabled us to explore the way in which the quest for the forgiveness of sins through the exercise of integrative power – the standing alongside the other with their memory of pain - can lead to new creation, and could help communities break through the thraldom of their memories of alienation.

It may be felt, by asking questions like these of the churches, that one is begging the question of the need for an expression of forgiveness in our societies. The whole thrust of this paper, however, has been to suggest that forgiveness of sin in the realm of human activity is the unique contribution of Jesus Christ in trying to free people so that they can live now. Christians cannot seek forgiveness or grant forgiveness on behalf of others. What they can do is to so live as a community of forgiveness that other views are challenged. That is the 'sign' character of the church. In living as 'sign' or 'sacrament' of God's presence through exhibiting 'integrative power', the Christian and the Christian community challenge other forms of the expression of power, destructive power above all. This suggests that it is not adequate to speak so easily of the powerlessness of the Church. Rather one needs to proclaim the rather unique insight of the Christian tradition which has seen and experienced a power which alone can enable people to be, above all though the power of forgiveness, and which alone can herald the new and break the cycle of "revengeful dust" (Edwin Muir), not by "circumventing history" but by taking "from that which made us that which will make us again."

NOTES

A first draft of this paper was presented at the Oxford consultation of the Forgiveness and Politics Project, associated with the British Council of Churches, July 1985.

1.  Edwin Muir *Collected Poems* London, Faber 1960, p 105.
2.  W.B. Yeats 'Vacillation' in *The Poems* ed. R. Finneran, Dublin, Gill and Macmillan, 1983, p 251.
3.  W.H. Auden *For the Time Being* London, Faber 1945; T.S. Eliot 'The Waste Land' in *Selected Poems* London, Faber 1954, p 51 ff. and 'East Coker' in his *Four Quartets* London, Faber 1959, p 23ff. T.S. Eliot's 'Little Gidding', like Edwin Muir's poems, moves to a more theological affirmation as the way in which this cyclic pattern is broken.
4.  Séamus Heaney *Preoccupations:* Selected Prose 1968-1978 London, Faber 1984 p 21.
5.  In my own congregation in Dublin which has given some 10% of its income to Christian Aid over the past year, there is a growing sense of frustration at the EEC grain surplus and Ireland's inability to increase its development aid contribution in terms of percentage of G.A.P. – evidenced by over half the congregation signing a petition to local T.D.s pressing for government action.
6.  For 'anomie' see Max Scheler *Resentiment* New York, Schocken Books 1972 p69f. 'angst' – see Soren Kierkegaard's writings.
7.  Edwin Muir 'The Annunciation' in *Collected Poems* op. cit. p117. A similar resolution for T.S. Eliot is evident in his 'Little Gidding' – *The Four Quartets* op.cit. The preoccupation of Muir with the theme of Journey, The Way, The Road, is also evidence of the possibility, for him, of change, movement, and power.

    A rather too brief acquaintance with Irish poetry suggests to me that this sense of the ability to move, or change is largely absent. As far as I can see only the early sagas, and the writings of Patrick Kavanagh and Seamus Heaney offer any vision of the ability to break with the past and shape the future. The cyclic constriction appears as the main theme of Brian Friel's recent play *Translations* London, Faber 1981.
8.  Hannah Arendt *The Human Condition* Chicago, Chicago Univ. Press 1958 pp236-247.
9   Monika Hellwig 'Christology and Attitudes toward Social Structures' in Thomas E. Clarke (ed.) *Above Every Name:* The Lordship of Christ and Social Systems, New York, Paulist 1980 p13f.
10. Paul Tillich blames the Ritschlian school of theology for this as they contrasted the love of God with his power in such a way that power disappeared and God became identified with love in its ethical meaning. See his *Love, Power and Justice* New York, O.U.P. 1954 p11f.
11. Otto Weber *Foundations of Dogmatics* trans. Darrell Goder 2 vols. Grand Rapids, Eerdmans 1981.
12. Commission on World Mission and Evangelism. *Your Kingdom Come:* Mission Perspectives, Geneva, WCC 1980.
13. Paul Tillich *Love, Power and Justice* New York, O.U.P. 1954; Karl Rahner *Theology of Power* Baltimore 1966.
14. Paul Tillich op.cit. p.45.
15. Friedrich Nietzsche *Werke* III p.468. The same motif is central to his *Thus Spoke Zarathustra* Harmondsworth, Penguin 1961.
16. Jacob Burckhardt *Welgeschichtliche Betrachtungen* p. 131, quoted and trans. by Jan Lochman in an unpublished lecture 'Thine is the Power: The Power of God and the God of Power' p.1.
17. Paul Tillich op.cit. p.41.
18. cf. the work of Jean Piaget.
19. Paul Tillich *The Courage To Be* Glasgow, Collins Fontana 1962.
20. Rollo May *Power and Innocence* Glasgow, Collins Fontana 1976 p.20f. The author is a psychotherapist in New York. At the 1982 Conference of the Catholic Theological Society of America John Coleman, in a keynote address, gave a similar analysis of power, drawing also on the work of Rollo May. He defined power as the capacity to sustain a relationship – influencing and being influenced; giving and receiving, etc. *C.T.S.A. Proceedings* 1982 pp 1-14.
21. Rollo May op.cit. pp 40-45.
22. Erich Fromm *The Fear of Freedom* London, RKP 1960 p.139; for a more delineated examination of aggressiveness see Erich Fromm *The Anatomy of Human Destructiveness* London, Jonathan Cape 1974 pp 185-218, and the Epilogue.

23. Erich From *The Fear of Freedom* op.cit. p.139.

24. Rollo May op.cit. pp 105-110. Even with this positive category of nutrient power, however, it is possible that a destructive effect may occur. The exercise of nutrient power could lead to dependence or to paternalism – factors which Rollo May seems to leave out of account.

25. This ambivalence in the use of power also applies to Christians and the Churches, as we take part in what Gregory Baum terms 'the ambiguity' of Christianity, and what David Jenkins calls '*The Contradiction of Christianity*' (London SCM 1976).

26. See Willy Brandt (Chairman) *North-South:* A Programme for Survival London, Pen Books 1980, especially the chapter on 'Mutual Interests' pp 64-77a. My colleague, Bill MacSweeney, in a recent article argues this as the principle of coherence for a nation's foreign policy; see 'Morality and Foreign Policy' in D. Keogh (ed.) *Central America:* Human Rights and U.S. Foreign Policy, Cork, Cork University Press 1985.

27. John MacQuarrie *Principles of Christian Theology* 2nd edn. London, SCM 1977, p.209, p.225.

28. John MacQuarrie op.cit. p.348.

29. Geddes MacGregor *He Who Lets us Be:* A Theology of Love, New York, Seabury Press 1975, p. 15.

30. Matthew Ch. 1, v 23. Isaiah 8, vv 8, 10.

31. See my elaboration of this theme in 'Theological Reflection on Human Rights' *Understanding Human Rights:* an Interdisciplinary and Interfaith Study, Alan D. Falconer (ed.), The Irish School of Ecumenics, 1980.

32. In trying to enunciate the fact that Jesus seems to exercise integrative power, it is tempting to overlook those incidents in the Gospels where Jesus is portrayed as using force. I do not feel that I have managed yet to integrate these conflicting ideas. In making the attempt to do so, however, I have found Paul Tillich's analysis of power and force in *Love, Power and Justice* (op.cit. p.45ff) to be helpful. Tillich notes that that which is forced must preserve its own identity, otherwise it is not so much forced as destroyed. Power, he asserts, may need compulsion but only to act as a stimulus for being. It seems to me that on those occasions where Jesus is portrayed as exercising compulsion, it is to initiate a change so that the other might be freed from his or her own past in such a way that they can take responsibility for their own lives in the present.

33. Charles Williams *The Forgiveness of Sins* Grand Rapids, Eerdmans 1984 p.52ff. The same direction of thought is evident also in Eduard Schweizer *The Good News According to Matthew* Atlanta, John Knox Press 1975, in his commentary on Ch.4: 1-11.

34. Hannah Arendt op.cit. p.240.

35. Charles Williams op.cit. p.50f.

36. Hannah Arendt op.cit. p.241. The importance of the 'unexpected' response to such exercises of power has been highlighted as an essential measure in breaking the ties to the past and enabling people to be free by René Girard in his writings. See especially his *Violence and the Sacred. op. cit.*

37. Jürgen Moltmann *The Trinity and the Kingdom of God* trans. Margaret Kohl London, SCM 1981.

    See also Lucien Richard *A Kenotic Christology:* In the Humanity of Jesus the Christ, the Compassion of Our God. New York, University Press of America 1982; and Roy S. Anderson *Historical Transcendence and the Reality of God* Grand Rapids, Eerdmans 1975 p.179.

38. Roger Schutz. cf. Leo Tolstoy *Resurrection* N.Y., New America Library *1961.*

39. See the powerful expressions of forgiveness in Etty Hillesum *A Diary,* London, Triad Granada 1985.

40. See Max Thurian *Confession* London, Mowbray 1985.

41. Rowan Williams *Resurrection* London, Darton, Longman & Todd 1982 p.29. cf. also Stanley Hauerwas *A Community of Character:* Toward a constructive Christian social ethic. Notre Dame, Notre Dame University Press 1981.

42. Recent histories of the Reformation period by both Protestant and Roman Catholic writers point to the corruption of the Church at the time. See for example A.G. Dickens *The Counter Reformation*

London, Thames & Hudson 1968; Pierre Janelle *The Catholic Reformation* London, Collier-Macmillan 1971; A.D. Wright *The Counter-Reformation* New York, St. Martin's Press 1982; A.G. Dickens *Reformation and Society in Sixteenth Century Europe* London, Thomas and Hudson 1966.

43. See *Unitatis Redintegratio* (Decree on Ecumenism) Par.7. A similar statement was made by the General Assembly of the Presbyterian Church in Ireland in 1966.

44. The irreconcilable attitudes to church polity led to the failure of The Covenant scheme in England and Wales, have led to serious difficulties with the Multilateral Conversations in Scotland, and caused tensions within the Anglican Communion when the Church of South India was established having reconciled these polities.

45. The 'sine qua non' nature of episcopacy is an assumption of Vatican II's *Lumen Gentium* and *Unitatis Redintegratio*. Such a view seems to many of the Reformed tradition to be explicit in the W.C.C. statement *Baptism, Eucharist and Ministry* (the Lima Report) as for example the response by the Church of Scotland.

46. In Mark Santer (ed.) *Their Lord and Ours* London SPCK 1982.

# Forgiveness and Community

*Gabriel Daly*

Recent interest in the theme of politics and forgiveness raises certain basic questions both about the concept of forgiveness itself and about how groups can practise it. This paper is an attempt to examine both questions. My title is therefore initially disjunctive. I am making no assumptions about the possibility and character of communitarian (including political) forgiveness. Instead I shall concentrate on the nature and scope of forgiveness in itself with a view to asking subsequently whether and how a community as such can forgive. I have found myself both drawn to the idea of political forgiveness and puzzled by its semantic implications. Can a community be said to forgive in the way that one individual forgives another; I shall argue that the most fruitful approach to this question is through analogy; but even with this in mind we are left with the further question of whence one derives the dominant or control model. I shall in fact derive it from individual interpersonal relationship, and I do so in full awareness of the severe critique of liberal individualism made by political theologians.

I agree with the main lines of this critique, including its summons to exchange the privacies of pietistic and existentialist subjectivism for the objective realities of social and political concern. Nevertheless I cannot help concluding that in our necessary attempts to give a social and political reference to the language of traditional Christian theology we run the twofold risk of (a) excessive reaction against personalism, and (b) equivocation in the use of certain traditional terms, especially those employed in soteriology. The word 'forgiveness', in my submission, provides a relevant instance of both risks.

First there is the tendency to take 'forgiveness' as a functional synonym for 'reconciliation' and 'atonement', whereas it is a more specific word than either. Alienation or estrangement can occur for reasons which do not necessarily include a specific offence or specific offences for which forgiveness needs to be sought or granted, even implicitly. 'Reconciliation' is arguably the most generic term in the vocabulary of soteriology. It correlates antithetically with 'alienation', which in the modern world is a word with both Marxian and Freudian associations. Theologians in their perfectly defensible quest for cultural relevance will almost inevitably wish to admit resonances from either or both into their thinking. In both cases, however, they must reckon with a rejection of transcendence which makes Marxian and Freudian thought not merely circumstantially but radically reductionist. Both Marx and Freud put forward a secularist soteriology in which there is no place for forgiveness. Christian soteriologies which admit Marxian or Freudian resonances have therefore to take this absence of the concept of forgiveness under conscious consideration and control.

*Forgiveness and Analogy*

F.W. Dillistone in his classic study, *The Christian Understanding of Atonement,*[1] warns against investing any single word, especially one from the vocabulary of soteriology, with the authority to embody an immediately agreed meaning or to evoke a standard response.

> The reconciliation about which I speak may not be an answer to the precise problem of estrangement with which my neighbour is concerned.[2]

We need, says Professor Dillistone, to examine 'the general framework within which the language of estrangement and reconciliation gains meaning'. Most of the major soteriological terms are analogical models linguistically signalized by metaphors. While the ability to create metaphor is one of the glories of the human imagination, we should not underestimate the equally human and perverse capacity for driving metaphors too hard and too far in the direction of univocacy, with consequent destruction of their original power to suggest what Paul Ricoeur has called a 'surplus of meaning'.[3]

Univocation occurred early in Christian theology when the Fathers, for example, took the text, 'The Son of Man came not to be served but to serve and to give his life as a ransom for many' (Mk 10:45) and asked the semantically fatal question, 'To whom was the ransom paid?'. It was a question which drove a fine and evocative metaphor on to the rocks of deficient sensibility. It was also a question which alerts us to the role of the imagination in the business of theological interpretation. There is what might be called an impressionistic ambiguity about some metaphors which even 'the loving inquisitiveness of the Schools' should leave undissected.

If classical Christian theology occasionally strayed in the direction of univocation in its theological language, post-Enlightenment theology has tended in the opposite direction, namely, towards equivocation. It continues to use classical terminology, but it risks using it in a manner and with a reference which evacuates the sense and reference of the original usage. Soteriology is especially vulnerable to this semantic drift. Dietrich Weiderkehr has remarked; 'Many of the traditional designations are to all appearances verbally retained and command the same respect as before, but they are really the vocabulary of psychology and the social sciences.' He goes on to ask provocatively, 'Can the Christian proclamation of salvation introduce its traditional revelation of sin and its promise of eternal healing into these new mediated experiences without adapting to an ephemeral vogue and yet without talking about something totally different and alien?'[4] I would wish to answer that question affirmatively, but only under the proviso of a carefully controlled methodology rooted in awareness of the analogical character of what is going on. Metaphors die if they are not given fresh reference; and if they die, they lapse into a pseudo-literalness which often distorts the original insight.

Analogy, however, is a wider concept than metaphor. Redemption, for example, is a soteriological model clearly signalized by a compressed metaphor. 'Reconciliation' and 'forgiveness' are not so obviously metaphorical, unless one is prepared to dig deep into their etymology. But the contextual reference of reconciliation and forgiveness is no less analogical than any of the other soteriological terms. Both receive their definitive meaning from the circumstances which bring them into play. Those circumstances can range from the trivial, e.g., forgetting a birthday or anniversary, to the cosmic horror of the Holocaust. One rarely speaks of forgiveness without some degree of ambiguity, if only because offence and culpability are not inseparable. We need 'forgiveness' also for our non-culpable offences against others, just as we need healing for the wounds which we incur simply by being human. Recognition of the analogical character of forgiveness becomes particularly important when divine and human forgiveness are related to each other and are invoked in the same context. With an uneasy glance towards the shade of Karl Barth, I would wish to argue that we know something about divine forgiveness from our experience of human forgiveness, its possibilities, and its limitations.

## Forgiveness as Transcendental

Can forgiveness be a purely secular reality quite devoid of transcendent reference or significance? The question will be important in any enquiry we may wish to make into communitarian or political forgiveness. I am not asking whether unbelievers can practise forgiveness. Obviously they can; but I would wish to argue that in doing so they give unwilling and perhaps unwitting testimony to the divine spark within them. An act of forgiveness may take place in a totally secular context and have no explicit or intended reference to God; but the believer is not thereby prohibited from seeing it as an ojective testimony to divine presence and action. It is not implausible to argue that the idea of forgiveness spontaneously suggests a religious context; and this fact may paradoxically militate against a recognition of its social and political implications. The introduction of forgiveness as an ideal into a political context may actually appear to rob that context of its secular autonomy; which in turn may lead the politically minded theologian to play down its transcendent reference. Forgiveness is not, in point of fact, a prominent feature in much political theology, presumably because it can seem to act as a brake upon revolutionary ardour. It is extremely difficult for a politician to speak of forgiveness, and sometimes even of reconciliation, without sounding like a preacher. There is, in short, something inescapably 'religious' about forgiveness and atonement. I should like to explore this contention with the help of a scene from Iris Murdoch's novel, *Bruno's Dream*.[5]

## Bruno's Dream

Bruno is nearly ninety. At several points in the novel we share in his confused musings on his past life, especially on his marriage to Janie. We learn of his single infidelity to her for which she had reproached him for the remainder of her life. Janie having discovered his affair, continues to live in the same house as Bruno but resolutely refuses to forgive him. She frequently commands him to her room there to berate him. One day Bruno hears the sound of her stick on the floor summoning him to her room for what he intuitively knows will be the last time. He does not go, because he cannot bear to hear her condemn him with her dying breath. The terrible decision has haunted him ever since. Bruno, it should be noted, is not religiously inclined. Very early in the story we are told that he 'had never bothered with religion, he had left that to the women, and his vision of goodness was connected not with God but with his mother'.[6] As the novel ends we find him, aware of his own imminent death, reflecting on his desperate desire for Janie's forgiveness and on his dread of being cursed instead. With the absolute clarity afforded by the prospect of his own death, Bruno reflects that 'if there is something that matters now at the end it must be the only thing that matters'.[7]

'If only it could work backwards, but it can't.'

Some people believed that too. That life could be redeemed. But it couldn't be, and that was what was so terrible. He had loved only a few people and loved them so badly, so selfishly. He had made a muddle of everything. Was it only in the presence of death that one could see so clearly what love ought to be like? If only the knowledge which he had now, this absolutely nothing-else-matters, could somehow go backwards and purify the little selfish loves and straighten out the muddles. But it could not.

Had Janie known this at the end? For the first time Bruno saw it with absolute certainty. Janie must have known. It would be impossible in this presence not to know. She had not wanted to curse him, she had wanted to forgive him. And he had not given her the chance.

'Janie, I am so sorry,' murmured Bruno. His tears flowed. But he was glad that he knew, at last.[8]

Bruno's dying reflections raise two questions which belong to eschatology and therefore to the transcendent dimension of history. First there is the clarity and truth made uniquely possible by the existential awareness of imminent death. Then there is the matter of how forgiveness can 'work backwards'. The prospect of death no merely concentrates the mind by removing most of the motives for duplicity, but in Bruno's case produces the insight that what matters at the end is the only thing that matters. He has of course to assume, on the basis of his own experience, that his wife Janie must have felt the same. For the dying Bruno this insight into the scope of forgiveness has the character of universality. As it is with him now, so it must have been with Janie. If one questions this universality, Bruno's conclusion can seem no more than wishful thinking.

It is, however, the implication that forgiveness must collapse the structure of timespace that most challenges us here. Forgiveness has indeed to 'work backwards' if it is to have universal value and purpose. If it is to mean anything, it needs to share somehow in the quality of eternity as Boethius understood eternity. It has to embrace the offence, the offender, and the offended in an act of 'total, complete, simultaneous possession'. Forgiveness, in short, is both a symbolic mediation of God and a transcendental experience arising out of human limitation. It both makes God present and, to the extent that even the most perfect expression of human forgiveness falls infinitely short of what it promises, stirs up a further longing for what is divinely possible. Bruno's phrase, 'working backwards', is a homely equivalent of what Helmut Peukert calls 'anamnestic solidarity' in his attempt to delineate a communications theory which is applicable to the entire human race, *past* as well as future. Historically the past is closed; eschatologically it remains open.[9]

## Ambiguity

There is in real forgiveness a divine-human ambiguity which makes it difficult to distinguish what is of God from what is of man. Forgiveness is an instance – perhaps the most challenging instance – of love, and as such it shares in the mystical ambiguity of the Johannine proclamation that 'God is love'. Whenever and wherever there is forgiveness, even of a totally 'secular' kind, there is God. This contention could offend not only unbelievers but also a certain type of Protestant and a certain type of Catholic sensibility. Protestants who are anxious to affirm the total sinfulness of men and women and their inability to contribute anything of their own to the salvific process will not wish to accept any blurring of the boundaries between divine and human action in matters to do with salvation. In the Roman Catholic tradition there has been a similar disposition to interpret grace ('actual grace') as a sort of divinely imparted moral shove against the grain and in the direction of true Christian behaviour. A juridical attitude to forgiveness, such as that which has characterized much Neo-scholastic Catholicism, reserves the transcendent dimension of forgiveness to the divine remission of sin normally mediated by divinely sanctioned ecclesial authority. Inter-human forgiveness is here seen merely as a moral act devoid of immanent, not to speak of numinous, significance. When forgiveness is treated sacramentally, and thus inserted into a formal ecclesiastical structure, it is also juridicized; the minister acts *in persona*

*Christi* but, from the standpoint of sacramental efficacy, with the impersonality and impassivity of a high court judge.

Ecclesiastical mediation of forgiveness has the almost inevitable effect of removing the spontaneity and intensity of God's offer of forgiveness as portrayed by Jesus. Much of the immediacy of the gospel paradigms is lost in circumstances which introduce an almost inevitable note of calculation common to all ecclesiastical mediation, from medieval penitentials to later confessional practice. The analogical relationship between human and divine forgiveness is easily obscured by socio-liturgical procedures, much as these aim to provide a social and ecclesial setting and reference. The Sermon on the Mount makes it abundantly and uncomfortably clear that inter-human forgiveness is a moral imperative with universal application. The gospel roots this universal imperative in the comprehensive generosity of divine forgiveness. What we have freely received must be freely, if analogously, distributed. Human forgiveness is an analogical mimesis of divine forgiveness; and love of enemies is its paradigmatic test. Many stratagems have been thought up for dealing with the angularities and attitudinal discomforts of the Sermon on the Mount. Such stratagems include the medieval distinction between the precepts and the counsels, the Lutheran doctrine of the Two Kingdoms, Schweitzer's idea of the interim ethic, and so on. It would be cynical to see in these stratagems only devices for attenuating the demands of the gospel. They are all genuine attempts to make the gospel relevant to life as it has to be lived in the world at any given moment. The New Testament, however, is not concerned, on the whole, to enter casuistically into circumstances by asking 'What if . . ?' It is concerned with a forgiving disposition which is to be always on call.

When Brendan Behan suggested that the first item on the agenda of any meeting of Irishmen was a split, he was being unduly nationalistic. A potential split ought to be taken as read on any human agenda. This is no more than a realistic recognition of what our theological ancestors were trying to say when they coined the term 'original sin'. It is both politically and theologically realistic to act on the assumption that there will be a split, and therefore to plan from the outset the means of damage control and subsequent bridge-building. This ought perhaps to be the Christian's most characteristic contribution to all social gatherings ranging from parochial committees to large-scale political enterprises. There is an unillusioned directness about the Letter to the Colossians: 'Be forbearing with one another, and forgiving, where any of you has cause for complaint: you must forgive as the Lord forgave you' (Col. 3:13).

A community of forgiveness is here envisaged as a community comprising individuals who accept forgiveness as an ideal to be practised in the ordinary and sometimes frictional exchanges of inter-human relationship. The problem for political theology (of the sort which is concerned about forgiveness) is how to give this network of interpersonal exchanges the impact of a block vote, and it raises once again the question of whether and how a community, as an entity, can be said to forgive in any sense which retains some measure of univocation. Is there a collective consciousness which can be said to be the subject of an act of forgiveness? We are faced here with all sorts of questions about how a group achieves solidarity of sentiment, especially of a sentiment like forgiveness which reaches into the depths of moral, psychological, and religious experience.

Forgiveness has a psychological dimension which is indispensable to its deepest meaning. By saying that I leave myself open to the charge of psychologism, i.e., of reducing forgiveness to its psychological element and of overlooking other no less important elements. Nevertheless this difficulty must be faced. It is for psychologists to indicate the possibility and character of group consciousness and to determine how that consciousness relates to the consciousness of the individuals who comprise the group. We are today reacting against the individualism and personalism of the romantic era; but such reaction is not a charter to abandon the inescapably individual and personal characteristics of a phenomenon such as forgiveness. Let us look, then, more closely at some of these characteristics, notably that of sacrifice.

*Sacrifice*
A reflection from Dag Hammarskjöld's journal offers a clue to the sacrificial character of forgiveness in its deeper reaches.

> Forgiveness breaks the chain of causality because he who "forgives" you – out of love – takes upon himself the consequences of what *you* have done. Forgiveness, therefore, always entails a sacrifice.[10]

In many cases such taking of consequences upon oneself calls for some kind of imaginative substitution, i.e., a placing of oneself in the offender's shoes. Take for example the case of parents of a child who has been killed by a drunken driver. Let us suppose that the offender has been courageous enough to face the parents and express his shame and contrition (having first ascertained the readiness of the parents to meet him). Let us further suppose that either or both of the parents feel that more is being asked of them than a dignified and brief encounter and an absence of overt recrimination. The sort of forgiveness which would be appropriate – though heroically so – to this situation would stem from their ability and willingness to override their own emotions sufficiently to imagine what it must be like to be a drunken driver who has killed a child and must now live with the consequences. Such imaginative substitution would rest partly on sheer human solidarity and partly on recognizing that the roles could be reversed without any serious straining of plausibility. The 'sacrifice' of which Hammarskjöld speaks would here consist not merely in conquering anger, disgust, loathing and all other rebarbative emotions natural in the circumstances, it would involve abandoning

105

the psychological solace offered by the indulgence of these emotions. It would no longer be possible to think of the driver as an unforgivable lout. Instead he would be invested with a 'redeemed' humanity which would make hatred of him impossible.

The example of the drunken driver may look like a case of special pleading in that it lends itself to imaginative transposition. If one were to choose instead an offence involving sheer malice, say, an act of deliberate slander, one would be forced to concede that the forgiving imagination would find it harder to function, even with the best of wills, simply because the would-be forgiver might not be able to make the imaginative leap into the subjectivity of the offender. Some kind of imaginative exchange of subjectivities, however, would seem to be necessary if politically estranged communities are to be reconciled. Their members have in some way to experience the implications of a common humanity. This will almost certainly mean reckoning not merely with the right of the other community but also with the lived experience of its members. Yet I have heard such imaginative exchange of subjectivities described as a kind of treason. When communities have been long estranged there has to be a shriving of memories (which enables the process to 'work backwards') and a shriving of dreams (which will come from the recognition that one community's dream may be the other's nightmare).

Does forgiveness, however, necessarily imply some kind of understanding of the offence? The question is important for at least two reasons. First there is, as I have suggested, the danger of a psychologism whereby one reduces the objective ontological character of sin to its purely psychological dimensions. Second, there is the danger of moral determinism. This could work on the principle *Tout comprendre, c'est tout pardonner*. Commenting on this slogan of deterministic behaviourism, Isaiah Berlin showed its derivation to lie not merely in moral determinism but actually in the whole western philosophical tradition from Plato onwards, and specifically in its conviction 'that reality is wholly knowable, and that knowledge and only knowledge liberates, and absolute knowledge liberates absolutely'.[11] In short that 'To explain is to understand and to understand is to justify'. Once again we are alerted to the analogical character of forgiveness. God's forgiveness of sin stems not from his omniscience but from his love. There is something objective to be forgiven, and no degree of psychological insight or moral empathy can remove that fact. Forgiveness is not synonymous with understanding, for either God or man, though there are instances where human forgiveness may depend on a willingness to understand as far as possible through the medium of the imagination; while in every instance it is only God who sees the heart.

The concept of forgiveness as a universal imperative has to face a far sterner test than that of avoiding psychological reductionism. Are there instances of crime so awesome in magnitude that they render the prospect of forgiveness both irrelevant and morally intolerable? The Holocaust puts the universal scope of forgiveness implicit in Christianity to its severest test. In the words of J-B. Metz one can no longer do theology with one's back to Auschwitz. Can one, however, face Auschwitz at a remove and yet with authenticity? What is abundantly clear is that those not directly involved must use the greatest circumspection in their invocation of forgiveness in this context. Perhaps the only sure course is to listen with painful humility to those who were directly affected.

## The Holocaust

Ulrich Simon is such a one, and he puts the case against forgiveness in the context of the Holocaust with deeply-felt conviction. He believes that 'our moral feelings tend to be outraged even by talk of forgiveness in this connection'.[12]

> There is a sin against Man and Spirit which Christ declared to be unforgivable, and Auschwitz is this sin against Man and Spirit. It is the supreme act of blasphemy, and the men and tools who caused it neither desire nor can receive the forgiveness of their sin.[13]

Although Professor Simon refuses to discuss Auschwitz in terms of forgiveness, he is ready to discuss it in terms of ultimate meaning. Where Richard Rubenstein was moved by the thought of Auschwitz to write that

> Few ideas in Jewish religious thought have been more decisively mistaken, in spite of their deep psychological roots, than the terrible belief that God acts meaningfully in history.[14]

Ulrich Simon is able to sanction the possibility of a theology of Auschwitz as long as 'it's findings issue in prayer, for we can face the horror only by coming to terms with it liturgically'.[15] Professor Simon's invocation of prayer in respect of Auschwitz suggests that such cosmic manifestations of evil have to be approached religiously or not at all, but that not even a religious approach permits one to speak of forgiveness in the case of such huge crimes against humanity. We are here dealing with events which lay bare the raw nerve ends of all that is ultimate in human concern. The problems posed for theodicy by the fact of Auschwitz are shattering, but our attention is directed here less to theodicy than to its implications for human forgiveness. Only those who were victims have the right to speak of forgiveness. For the rest of us it would be a gross impertinence. We are, however, entitled to enquire with reverence whether there were victims who did in fact forgive.

There is a prayer which comes not from Auschwitz but from Ravensbruck where 92,000 women and children died. This prayer is one of the miracles of religious history – almost as awesome as the conditions which produced it were numbing. Although it is now widely known and celebrated, I make no apology for citing it yet again.

O Lord, remember not only the men and women of good will, but also those of ill-will. But do not remember all the suffering they have inflicted on us; remember the fruits we have bought, thanks to this suffering – our comradeship, our loyalty, our humility, our courage, our generosity, the greatness of heart which has grown out of all this, and when they come to the judgement let all the fruits that we have borne be their forgiveness.[16]

In the light of that glorious prayer, offered by a nameless woman and placed beside the dead body of a nameless child, I would with respectful hesitancy question Professor Simon's claim that 'None of the victims at Auschwitz wrought atonement'.[17] Christians believe that there is only one mediator between God and man and that by his blood alone are we redeemed; but may one not speak of a mystical unity between Calvary and Ravensbruck when a victim of the latter reproduces so perfectly what the former was intended to effect? Pascal's remark that 'Jesus will be in torment until the end of time' gives us warrant to speak analogically of atonement in these circumstances. All that Jesus achieved on Calvary was present in the heart of that nameless woman in Ravensbruck, whether or not she was a Christian. Her prayer manifests the kingdom of God in all its splendour. In a sense it bridges the infinite distance between God and man. It is a manifestation of divinity which gives flesh and blood to the daring patristic conviction that God became man that man might become God. On Calvary man's inhumanity to man became in a unique way man's inhumanity to God, who responded not by annihilating his failed creation but by giving back to men and women the result of their sin transformed now into a sign of forgiveness and hope.

To see the figure on the cross as a symbol of forgiveness and reconciliation calls for an act of interpretation which can easily go unnoticed – precisely as interpretation – by believers, principally because tradition has already, as it were, made the interpretation for them. Even unbelievers share to some extent in the cultural implications of this socio-religious interpretation. The cross is inescapably associated with Christian culture, and that culture survives in considerable part into a secularist age. All of which makes it difficult for Christians to see the secular horror and degradation of Calvary and therefore to appreciate the demand it makes on the interpretative imagination. Without this act of Faith-inspired interpretation it is impossible to relate Calvary to Auschwitz or to any other manifestation of man's inhumanity to man. Among the many horrors inherent in the memory of Auschwitz is the fact that the persecutors were the lethal product of the long disease (much of it latent) of a Christian anti-semitism which was a denial of everything that Calvary represented. Repentance for Auschwitz implies repentance for every Christian manifestation of anti-semitism. This is yet a further reminder of the radically eschatological character of repentance and atonement.

We are surrounded in the world by the symbols of alienation and human offence.

The Christian is sent into the world to proclaim and live the values of the divine reign which Jesus proclaimed and incarnated. That proclamation has at its heart the assurance of God's forgiveness and the injunction to mediate in a human manner that divine forgiveness. In the risen Christ God gives humanity not merely a future it had no right to expect but a redeemed future, a future with hope, which it had still less right to expect. It was the crucified Christ who was raised in a divine act which transformed shame into glory. That forgiveness works not only backwards but forwards into both the historical and absolute future. It frees the forgiven for action on behalf of others. But it lays a radical obligation upon those who have responded in faith to the Father's raising of his murdered Son to new life: to be thus forgiven is to be both empowered and enjoined to forgive each other. Forgiveness is therefore at the heart of Christian community, however analogously it has to be practised. The Christian community is by definition and charter a community of forgiveness precisely because it is a forgiven community. How is this to be expressed in all the diverse circumstances in which Christians find themselves in the world? The remainder of this paper will be taken up with reflection on the communitarian character and implications of forgiveness.

*Summary*
Let me first, however, summarize some of my previous contentions. Forgiveness is neither an univocal nor an equivocal concept. It has to be approached with an analogical imagination capable of interpreting the facts of any situation which calls for reconciliation and the healing of wounds which have been inflicted by specific offences. It begins as a residual disposition which may be actualized at any moment and brought to bear on the ambiguities of the many situations which call it into play. These ambiguities include such considerations as culpability (e.g. diminished responsibility) and group solidarity (e.g. a community suffering guilt by association with its delinquent members). Forgiveness is analogical in that while its paradigmatic instance occurs in one-to-one relationships, it is the community which supplies the language for its identification and specification, and it is in the community that it has to be practised. Forgiveness is one of the principal signals of transcendence – a contention which seems to be borne out by the difficulty of giving it an exclusively empirical and non-religious reference. Forgiveness is therefore eschatological in that it is a mark of the inbreaking kingdom of God. When true forgiveness occurs, there is God. This divine presence is ontological and symbolic and not merely juridical or psychological. For the Christian the reality of forgiveness is ultimately tested by the paradigmatic instance of love of one's enemies, which is psychologically impossible in many cases if one is not prepared to undertake some kind of imaginative substitution. This imaginative substitution becomes particularly important in the case of alienated communities. Finally, one has to ask whether some offences are so enormous that they cannot be forgiven

because they destroy the language which invests forgiveness with meaning and reference. This question may be answered in the negative as long as one does so with extreme sensitivity to what is involved.

## The Forgiving Community

To call the Christian Church a community of forgiveness is arguably to veer towards the equivocal element in analogical predication. Is one speaking empirically, eschatologically, ontologically, or juridically? Is one describing the local community or the catholica? Is one speaking of divine or human forgiveness? The ambiguities inherent in the phrase 'community of forgiveness' strain analogy to its limits. Yet one is hardly free to despair of discovering a univocal element. Without a firm if limited element of univocation analogical interpretation would be impossible and therefore rational discourse about forgiveness would be impossible. There is, however, the lexical reference of the word from which we can at least make some sort of provisionally univocal start. 'To cease to resent', 'to pardon', 'to remit' are dictionary synonyms. They at least provide a context in ordinary universal and non-theological experience. The challenge to christian theology is how to relate this human experience to God's self-disclosure and action in the world. I have already intimated my own preference for an ontological and symbolic centre of reference: Where there is forgiveness, there is God. It does not matter where or between whom this forgiveness occurs. When it does occur, the divine element in men and women is activated. How one relates this to the work of Christ is a christological problem of daunting complexity. Karl Rahner's concept of the 'anonymous Christian' is a brave but unsatisfactory attempt to link the universality of divine grace with the specific limitations of a particular historical faith. The universal scope of forgiveness has often been severely attenuated in Christian history by a rigid doctrine of predestination or by a rigid application of the dictum *Extra ecclesiam nulla salus,* both of which appear to negate the universality of divine forgiveness and to sever the link between divine and human forgiveness. In both instances the community of forgiveness becomes a segregated, tightly-knit association of believers no longer interested in the universal character of forgiveness.

Rosemary Haughton in her book, *The Transformation of Man: A Study of Conversion and Community,* examines two communitarian responses to the divine offer of salvation in Christian history. She calls them respectively 'the community of the transformed' and 'the formation community'. The transformed community is well exemplified in the 17th century groups of radical Protestants who found themselves unable to live and worship according to their consciences under the Stuarts. Many of these Separatists set up communities abroad. They afford a clear example of how a group of Christians, conscious of being called out of a sinful world by a conversion experience, organized their daily lives in autonomous

110

communities. Mrs Haughton praises their fervour, devotion, and charismatic gifts but regrets their rigidity, smugness, and occasional hypocrisy.

The second type of response to the offer of salvation is the 'formation community', of which Mrs. Haughton takes the Benedictines as being a typical example. Here salvation has been traditionally seen as lying in the future. It has to be striven for. The virtues of this type of community are humility, respect for authority and for the material things that make life and worship together. Its defects are that its members 'are wide open to minimalism and tepidity, to evasion of personal responsibility and flight from decision'.[18]

Mrs Haughton convicts both types of community of confusing the sacred and the secular. 'One way imposes behaviour proper to contact with the sacred as the norm of secular life, the other treats secular life as if it were sacred.'[19] She believes that true Christian community would keep sacred and secular 'distinct *and* related'.

In terms of forgiveness it might be said that the transformed community had the better theology: The Christian ideal is to set out to forgive one another because we have been forgiven by God. There is however the problem of post-conversion sin which troubled the early Church, as it must trouble any community which lives in the light of an unrepeatable conversion experience. The formation community did not have this problem, since it acted on the assumption that salvation has to be worked for under grace across a lifetime marked by some success and much failure. The formation community expected failure and planned accordingly. Before the change of consciousness brought about in the Roman Catholic Church by the Second Vatican Council the formation community, living under rule and vows, set out to live a 'more perfect life' by practising the evangelical 'counsels' which were not deemed to bind the wider Christian community.[20] The formation community promoted constant renewal of effort and conversion, but conversion did not feature prominently in its vocabulary and was rarely if ever thought of as a decisive unrepeatable moment. Recent reforms have not changed this attitude. Although conversion has today a much more prominent role in Roman Catholic spirituality, it is normally understood as a continuing process and not as an unrepeatable event.

The formation community is typically Catholic in that it tends to sacralize power, to display theocratic pretensions, and to attach disproportionate significance to the mediation of God's mind and will through Church authority. It allows generously for human weakness, but it does so by appearing to regulate divine forgiveness, rather in the spirit of the parent who takes the gift box of chocolates away from the child with the purpose of doling out the contents under conditions of prudent control. The transformed community, on the other hand, aims at a spirituality of all-encompassing and non-calculating intensity. It protests at the intrusive character of Catholic ecclesial mediation. It allows the child to keep the chocolates, but on the understanding that the child will behave like an adult. If the child does not behave like an adult, the system breaks down and even logic itself may be infringed by attempts to demonstrate that the signs of salvation are present. (This illustration has literal reference when we remember that the Separatists sometimes beat their children to make them look more saved. St Benedict beat his 'in order that they may be cured'.[21] The children, of course, found both eschatologies equally painful.)

Roman Catholicism places heavy emphasis on the sacramental manifestation of divine forgiveness with consequent ecclesiastical control over its mediation. Protestantism removes the mediation with consequent privatization of the whole process. Neither appears to affirm the ontological, if analogical, unity of divine and human forgiveness. Without this unity it is difficult to create a realistic community of forgiveness, that is, a community which lives out divine forgiveness by expressing it analogically in interpersonal and social relationships and in a network of symbols designed to manifest the inner aspiration to forgiveness and to evoke it by outward sign.

There is a christological implication in all this, 'Who can forgive sins but God alone?' (Mk.2:7) was the theological objection brought by the authorities against Jesus's offer of forgiveness to the paralysed man. Some Christian apologists, by an extrinsic coupling of the forgiveness with the subsequent miraculous healing, utilized this text as proof of Jesus's divinity. They were, however, unwilling to accept that the divine forgiveness was rooted in the *human* compassion which Jesus felt for sinners. They thus neglected the gospel evidence that both the healing and the forgiveness were motivated by human compassion. Monophysites and Nestorians, each in their different ways, accepted the premiss of Jesus's accusers, the former deriving the forgiveness from a single, divine, nature in Christ, the latter affirming two natures but attributing forgiveness only to the divine. The consequence of Chalcedonian doctrine has been the depreciation of the human element in divine forgiveness, making human forgiveness less an extension of, than a heteronomous adjunct to, divine forgiveness.

In Roman Catholic Neo-scholastic theology and spirituality the radical distinction made between nature and supernature promoted the heteronomy. Love of neighbour was undertaken *propter Deum,* and this could subtly turn the neighbour into the raw material for one's acts of charity. (I am not suggesting that only Neo-scholastics practised this spiritual pragmatism, merely that their doctrine of nature and supernature gave it a theoretical underpinning.) The words of Jesus about care for those in need as described in the 25th chapter of Matthew's Gospel were frequently interpreted: 'As long as you did it to one of these, I took it as though you were doing it to me'. Eduard Schweizer's defiant anti-mysticism puts him curiously close to the old Neo-scholastic supernaturalists:

> We are therefore dealing neither with mysticism, in which the line between God and man is blurred, nor with Stoic identification of God with all mankind, but

with an act of charity to a particular individual who may not be appealing or sympathetic.[22]

Against both supernaturalism and moralism I wish to argue for the immanent, if imperfect, presence and manifestation of divine forgiveness in human forgiveness. The recognition that Jesus's acts of forgiveness were divine acts in a human mode and were inspired by human compassion can be made the christological basis of communitarian forgiveness (assuming, of course, that one accepts some form of incarnational christology). Karl Barth, redoubtable opponent of *analogia entis* that he was, could nevertheless write,

> It is when we look at Jesus Christ that we know decisively that God's deity does not exclude, but includes his *humanity*.[23]

What are the political implications of all this for Christians? Since politics is about how society sets up communicative structures and organizes itself for government, the political process almost inevitably entails the giving of offence. A split on the agenda is implicit in all political process. The Christian who engages in this process can scarcely claim that the hard facts of political life dispense him or her from any attempt to practise forgiveness in the political arena. Politicians are not dispensed by the exigencies of a public life from the demands of interpersonal morality. What, however, about the social and political embodiment of forgiveness? Is it, or can it be, something more than the sum of the individual attitudes of its members?

Though political action can certainly create symbols of forgiveness, it cannot compel individual citizens to participate internally in these symbols and in the reality to which they point. Internal participation is nevertheless a necessary feature of forgiveness in its deepest and characteristically Christian sense. Laws and administrative procedures can indeed reduce the occasions for offence and can penalize *external* manifestations of prejudice and hatred; but they cannot produce the inner disposition which is the heart of unfeigned forgiveness. The will to forgiveness in a group depends on the disposition which each of its members brings to the group. This fact makes forgiveness different from most other kinds of reforming social action. Social and political reforms can be brought about without any inner disposition towards forgiveness or reconciliation on the part of those affected by the reforms.

To question the spiritual limitations of politics does not imply the view that politics is an essentially sinful activity, or at least more sinful than other human activities. It simply means recognizing the danger of political reductionism and serves as a further reminder that there are limits to the scope of analogy in applying the concept of forgiveness. Forgiveness, more than anything else, demonstrates both the need and the limitations of political action. Bringing in legislation which will serve to reduce the occasions of community hostility is altogether desirable and laudable; but it is not forgiveness. It may indeed help to create an atmosphere favourable to forgiveness, but law and public administration are concerned with external actions not, directly at least, with interior dispositions. This is not to disparage the benefits of political initiative in matters of social antagonism. It is merely to recognize the transcendental character of forgiveness. As Aristotle pointed out in a different context, the virtues of the good citizen are not necessarily those of the good man.

However much we politicize our theology there always remains an area of religious concern which *finally* escapes the influence of politics; and forgiveness in its gospel sense belongs to this area. Lest this remark be taken to imply acquiescence in false consciousness, I must emphasize that I am presupposing preliminary political action which does what it can in the public arena before going on to reflect on the interior deficiencies inherent in that arena.

Charles Davis has remarked with admirable clear-sightedness that just as mysticism without politics is false consciousness, so politics without mysticism is 'mere business'.[24] It is 'only when Christians as Christians engage in politics that they experience the transcendent reality of God as limiting the political.'[25] The politics of reconciliation is particularly open to transcendental experience precisely because, if entered into from a genuine concern for peace and justice, it poses questions about human nature and its God-directed dynamism which politics is incompetent to answer. It is when this 'limit situation' is reached that forgiveness in its Christian sense becomes possible. The will to reconciliation may begin as a vague desire to end hostilities or make the neighbourhood safer, and as such it is enormously important and beneficial. The task of the Christian, however, is to extend the process inwards into the hearts of men and women where it ceases to be 'mere business' and becomes an exercise in bringing about the kingdom of God.

## NOTES

This paper was also delivered to the joint meeting of the Irish Theological Association and the Society for the Study of Theology in Belfast, April 1986.

1. F.W. Dillistone, *The Christian Understanding of Atonement* (Welwyn, 1968).
2. Dillistone, op.cit., p.12.
3. P. Ricoeur, *Interpretation Theory: Discourse and the Surplus of Meaning*, (Fort Worth, 1976), passim.
4. D. Weiderkehr, *Belief in Redemption: Concepts of Salvation from the New Testament to the Present Time* (London, 1979), p.48.
5. I. Murdoch, *Bruno's Dream* (Penguin Books, London, 1970).
6. Murdoch, op.cit., p.13.
7. Ibid., p.266.
8. Ibid., p.267.
9. H. Peukert, *Science, Action, and Fundamental Theology: Towards a Theology of Communicative Action* (Cambridge, Mass., 1984).
10. D. Hammarskjöld, *Markings* (London, 1966), p.163.
11. I. Berlin, *Historical Inevitability* (London, 1954), pp. 41-2.

12. U. Simon, *A Theology of Auschwitz* (London, 1978), p.66.
13. Simon, op.cit., p.71.
14. D. Callahan (ed.), *The Secular City Debate* (London, 1966), p.142.
15. Simon, op.cit., p.47.
16. Cited in M. Craig, 'Take Up Your Cross', *The Way,* Vol.13 (Jan., 1973), p.30.
17. Simon, op.cit., p.90.
18. R. Haughton, *The Transformation of Man: A Study of Conversion and Community* (London, 1967), p.240.
19. Haughton, op.cit., p.241.
20. T. Matura, *Gospel Radicalism: The Hard Sayings of Jesus* (Dublin, 1984) provides a convincing rebuttal of this view once widely accepted in Roman Catholic spirituality.
21. *Rule,* ch.30.
22. E. Schweizer, *The Good News According to St Matthew* (London, 1975), pp.477-8.
23. K. Barth, *The Humanity of God* (London, 1967), p.46, original italics.
24. C. Davis, *Theology and Political Society* (Cambridge, 1980), p.181.
25. Davis, op.cit., p.68.

# Reconciliation: An Ecumenical Paradigm

*Maurice Bond*

## Introduction

The central fear in much of our modern ecumenical and perhaps political debates is that of a loss of *identity* and this is as keenly felt here in Ireland as anywhere. It is not, for the most part, a fear of leaving the truth behind because most of us realise that the truth moves out beyond our traditions but one of being lost – the failure to preserve – something particular and important in our self-understanding. Our traditions are important to us, therefore, not simply because we believe them to be vehicles of truth but because they are our traditions – because they are vehicles of meaning. Truth claims are important – vital in terms of Christian belief – but in praxis they are often directed by our need to preserve that identity.

If our conception of identity and its preservation is static and reactionary then in a pluralist context it will also be conflictual.

Our task in this paper will be to examine the nature of identity and its preservation by way of a more dynamic paradigm which, if given any credence, would demand *conversation* between traditions as a way of preserving those traditions themselves. We will attempt to examine these concepts by way of some recent developments in phenomenology and hermeneutical studies. The fundamental catagories being *belonging; distance, conversation* and *fusion of horizons*. How these terms are being used can only fully emerge in the course of this paper.

## Section One

### The Ontological Reality of Pluralism

Martin Heidegger's work is central to this whole area. Heidegger's thesis is that ontology precedes and bases reflective understanding. Much of modern science proceeds on the assumption of a subject-object split in reality. Within such thinking the knowing subject examines objectivity or 'otherness' as that which exists over against subjectivity while for Heidegger thinking arises out of a context in which both subject and object are already bound together in being.

What is involved here can be seen clearly against the background of the philosophy of Descartes. Descartes begins with his famous *Cogito-ergo-sum* (I think therefore I am) which proceeds via the doubting of everything outside of the ego itself towards certainty which is based on the first principle of *Res cogitans* and moves forward by *Res existens*. This naked existing ego from which he begins is not first of all placed in being but rather can be shown to exist because it perceives itself as existing. In this way Descartes exemplifies the subject/object dichotomy of much of modern thought. The subject begins by distancing himself from that which he seeks to know. The first characteristic of his environment is its otherness in the form of dichotomy.

In contrast Heidegger seeks to explicate the reality of *Da-sein* (there-being). Our first and primary consciousness of ourselves is not of subject over against object but of inhabiting a world, a world which contains our traditions and those of others. In this way understanding is seen as being 'wordly' in that it arises from our recognition of being placed in being. This giveness of the world we inhabit as a predetermined starting point is characterized by Heidegger as our facticity *(faktizitat)*. The world we inhabit is part of our self consciousness. The naked existing ego does not in fact exist at all but is rather an abstraction from existential reality. All understanding proceeds from and is directed by being itself – that within which we are as what we are. The explication of something as this or that is founded upon our forehaving, foresight and foreconception *(vor-habe, vor-sicht, vor-griffe)*. All knowledge is anticipated by this basic pre-understanding of being placed.

Not only do we reason from our place but we reason back to it. This is the hermeneutical circle which rightly understood, relates me back to my place in being with new possibilities expanding that world itself. That world is not, therefore, expanded or challenged by an attempt to reason out of my place into that of another but is only meaningful in the existential sense if it returns and enlightens my world. It will never be academic in the sense of seeing itself as cut loose from significance for *Da-sein*. Understanding is always application in this sense. This will be of vital importance when we come to examine what it means to understand 'another' tradition.

It is Hans-Georg Gadamer who extends these observations and brings out their fuller implications as they apply to tradition and its authority. According to Gadamer, the overapplication of the modern scientific consciousness is in danger of alienating man from the fundamental recognition of 'belonging'. This is true in the field of art, history and literature. Both art and language are historical realities and man cannot meaningfully relate to history as an object over against himself but only as that to which he belongs. Before we take hold of history, history takes hold of us. There is no objective knowledge of history but only that kind of knowledge which arises from and returns to the situation in which subject and object are already bound together in their being. Language is historical and our place within the context of our language is itself a central characteristic of our historicity. It also, therefore, lays hold of us before we lay hold of it as the medium of our understanding. Understanding can be described in this way as linguistic.

These observations prompt Gadamer to a reappraisal of what he calls *the enlightenment's prejudice against prejudice*[1] which typifies the modern methodological division between bare subjective reason and 'objective being'. In so doing it attempts to reason from a non-place. Prejudice understood as pre-understanding or understanding funded by our tradition is a reality which cannot be suspended or denied because it is part of the forestructure of the process of understanding. The enlightenments attack on prejudice is aimed at what it considers to be the negative force of tradition which it considered to be a force which binds reason to dead and deadening convention and which prevents it from meaningful progression. While Gadamer would agree that in a real sense we are bound up with tradition and that it has indeed such an effect when simply repeated, he would as we shall see, reject the notion that the latter need be the case and would insist that interpretation as opposed to mere repetition is the one way in which man may have a real sense of belonging in his historically constituted world.

But how does tradition constitute itself as the place of reasoning – the context of understanding? Here he points to what he calls "effective historical consciousness". The consciousness which is one of being exposed to history as historical beings. This history to which we are exposed and in which we live is constituted by event, meaning and effect. Tradition includes all of this and in our being bound to that tradition we ourselves are part of its history as it is part of us.

Gadamer sees his task as the rehabilitation of tradition as such and it is not his primary task to examine how traditions might relate to each other within the context he describes. Nevertheless, it is not tradition with which we are bound up but traditions, not only culture but cultures, not only language but languages. Not only do we inhabit the world but worlds. Within Christianity itself – and this is the nub of the matter for us – we are constituted in our being by and grounded in different traditions from which reasoning proceeds and to which it returns.

The importance of all this is not that it brings about a recognition that no interpretation of anything is without presuppositions. This is fact long since taken for granted in hermeneutical studies at least if not yet in scientific research which often imagines itself to be in the world of objective knowledge. Rather, the real importance of the works of both Heidegger and Gadamer lies in their explication of the nature of these presuppostions as predispositions which are grounded not just in epistemology but in ontology. They are not just a starting point from which we proceed to understand and evaluate but what we are and that to which understanding brings us back with expanded possibilities for selfhood – "our ownmost possibilities".[2]

Thinking which is aware of its own historicity is thinking which is aware of its finitude. The related concepts of prejudice and effective historical consciousness belong to an ontology of finitude. In that our way of knowing is bound up with our particular tradition and the prejuduce which being in that tradition entails we cannot place ourselves in an a-historical position which would give us an all seeing overview or an infinite perspective. Such a perspective would demand the finding of a non-existent vantage point in being.

The question now arises, how is ecumenics to proceed – what can unity or identity mean amidst this pluralism? Do our prejudices and the effective historical consciousness which places us within our tradition mean that our place is fixed or static? On this basis ecumenical conversation would indeed be impossible and any attempts to converse would be a repeating of immobile positions across unbridgeable divides. This is why, for example, Protestant fundamentalists and Catholic ultra conservatives find ecumenics on anything more than a cosmetic basis nonexistent. If, on the other hand, we are forced forward from this static position by the needs of real *conversation* with our own traditions, then the same forward movement should involve the ecumenical conversation as well.

Having considered the phenomenon of belonging we must go on to say that this belonging displays an internal complexity. The way in which we belong to our traditions is described by Gadamer as the polarity of familiarity and strangeness. Our tradition is made up of texts and symbols, many of which are distanced from us in time and space – we belong to them and they to us within the tension of the near and the far. Many of these texts are historically intended in the sense of addressing a particular situation in a particular time. Effective historical consciousness means that we have a connection with the tradition out of which and to which these texts spoke and speak. Yet they are different from us in that we are now in a different situation which has new questions and a plurality of answers in the contempory context. This pluralist world is also part of our situation in being along with all its traditions – religious and political. We are, therefore, faced with two possibilities – an unreal and a real one. The unreal situation is that we may attempt to live in the past world which lies behind the text or our present situation. In which case there is no real communication with our tradition much less with another in a way which might provide us with the possibility of being challenged and challenging the modern perspectives of our time by the retrieval of meaning from these texts or history. We are content rather to ignore contemporary questions – including the pluralist question – and concentrate instead on a vain attempt at temporal regression. The real possibility is for a progressive interpretation which expands and enriches our tradition by bringing its relevance into our situation and time. Here real conversation and communication are active not only within our own traditions *(intra-communication)* but also with other traditions *(inter-communication)*. The human encounter with the world is a never finished process and progression of meaning and human experience gives rise to ever new encounters with our traditions.

The task of hermeneutics is to address itself to this tension of belonging and distance or, to put it another way, these two senses of belonging. If we are to *preserve* our traditions we must do so by interpreting them in a dynamic way. What David Tracy would call 'radical belonging', which is radical in two senses – towards tradition and by the retrieval of meaning via tradition towards the present for the future. It is in this light that the concept of horizon assumes a central significance for Gadamer.

We are constantly being re-informed. The hermeneutical circle thus proves to be an expanding rather than a vicious one. A return to self with enlarged vision and being. No disloyalty to our traditions is involved on the contrary only thus can we really maintain them. Thus, just as ecumenics is impossible on the basis of static traditionalism, so is loyalty to our own traditions.

But can we go further still by explicating how this loyalty to and preservation of our own tradition can demonstrate the inherent necessity of and provide a model for the ecumenical task?

*Section Two*

### 1. The Ecumenical Significance of the Concept of Belonging

We have found via Heidegger and Gadamer that the concept of belonging to tradition is a central one in the recognition of our place within being. We have further noted the obvious fact that this belonging is pluralist – we do not all belong to the same tradition. The Christian tradition is represented in different traditions.

Now Christians of all ages have at all times insisted that the Church has an essential unity. Once we have accepted the historicity of our own positions and the finitude which this entails, we have accepted that no tradition can have an a-historical or absolute claim to truth. The task remains therefore as one of explicating the reality of Christian unity from a pluralist standpoint. We have suggested that this need brings us back to the problem of how we interpret tradition as such and our own tradition in particular. Our common recognition that despite the distance between us the universal belief in the unity of the Church entails common belonging as the body of Christ is the ecumenical spur. This belief comes to us from the heart of our own tradition – whatever that tradition may be – and in that it is this tradition which informs our prejudices of the ecumenical compulsion of Christian being as part of the facticity of being 'thrown' into a Christian tradition. This has immediate implications in that it means that all the texts and symbols of whatever tradition belong to all Christians. But it goes further than this for we belong to these texts and symbols at a distance. A distance which as we shall see is not only temporal but in the case of other traditions contemporary. It is a question now not just of intra-communion but inter-communion. This concept of contemporary distance will need further explanation. At this point we can say that it results from our being placed with different traditions and its reality is both an historical and contemporary fact. Nevertheless, just as our unity with our own traditions precedes our explication of it by laying hold of us before we lay hold of it so also our essential unity which enfolds these traditions is a fact before we recognise it. It is already even if it is not yet pursued or exercised. If different Christian traditions are part of that to which we belong and if we are not to return to the subject-object dichotomy, it follows that we cannot treat these 'different' traditions as objects overagainst us. We are dealing with that which is part of us within the effective historical consciousness of Christian unity (or Irish history?). In considering our essential belonging at a distance with the texts of tradition Gadamer uses the I-thou analogy not in respect to any person to person appeal but on the basis of being addressed by the meaningful content of the texts and symbols themselves. We are involved in that which we seek to interpret. This analogy functions in a similar way with regard to the ecumenical encounter with the text, myths and symbols of other traditions.

Within our horizons we have this consciousness of unity which involves a twofold tension of belonging and distance. We have looked at what this belonging means and can now examine more closely the other side of tension — distance.

These horizons have the 'near and the far' — our contemporary self-consciousness and our relationship, of belonging to texts and symbols which are distanced in time from us yet part of us as effective historical consciousness. The same horizons include a consciousness of unity with other traditions but again it is a unity with tensions. Not only is there the temporal tension because we are distanced from these 'other' traditions in time but the contemporary distance which arises out of our 'different' places or being placed within different traditions which while they include each other do so as identity-in-difference. The relationship has the character of being a dialectic which consists in these tensions. The aim of ecumenics is the explication and realisation of Christian unity within this dialectic. But how is this to be done? Does it consist in the neutralising of these tensions so that they disappear? We have suggested that this is not only impossible but undesirable because it would make it impossible for us to appropriate the Christian faith with relative adequacy to the diverse questions of human diversity and facticity. The real possibility lies, as with the interpretation of our own historical tradition in what Gadamer calls the 'fusion of horizons'. If we take for example, the South American Roman Catholic Church we find that how it experiences its needs may share certain similarities with the Western Church but also has differences. It is in a sense a tradition (South American) within a tradition (Roman Catholic) within a tradition (Christian) and shows how despite greater awareness of each other in our modern world the pluralist reality is heightened rather than lessened; no vain attempt at demolishing the differences between these traditions will succeed because such an attempt would fail to take account of the ontological realities and questions which arise from 'there-being' in that world. Nor can we in the west simply lift their tradition and set it into our context. Nevertheless the ecumenical encounter is an imperative of being the Christian Church and demands appropriation of the possible implications of Latin American theology by way of a 'fusion of horizons'.

## 2. The Ecumenical Significance of the Concept of the Fusion of Horizons

Two senses of 'preservation' can be distinguished but not separated. There is the way in which I preserve my tradition by rendering it meaningful to and in the contemporary context which includes other traditions. The second form of preservation is the way in which even in this identity there can be no capitulation of one horizon to the other for example, in interpreting the Christ event as it is portrayed through the gospels. I preserve my identity with the core of Christian tradition, but it must be a real interpretation and cannot be on the basis of attempting to repeat a first century mind or situation. My own position as a 20th century person asking 20th century questions must also be preserved. Interpretation is not repetition any more than identity means being identical. Gadamer's 'fusion of horizons' promises to explicate a more dialectical approach to identity which can fully take account of these two senses of preservation. It is not the forsaking of one place in order to be something else but an expansion of selfhood by way of being identified with and challenged by the 'other'. The same is true of the ecumenical encounter. (The political encounter as well?)

Interpretation and identity as a 'fusion of horizons' follows on from what we have said about prejudice. It is important to emphasize again that horizons cannot be rightly seen as a set of fixed and static opinion which render us unable to evaluate 'otherness' – they are rather the basis of a dynamic and expanding self-understanding. We are characterised not just by what we are but by possibility – what we might be. Being reaches out in front of us so that ontology is a quest as well as a present reality. In this way the unity of the Church partakes in the nature of being as such – it is already and not yet. As individuals and as communities we must constantly become ourselves in order to be ourselves. Each new experience of understanding must assimilate newness to what we are so that selfhood maintains a continuity in every new encounter with being. If our traditions are to enrich our present, they will do so by the process of retrieval of meaning for that present by hermeneutical interpretation. The retrieval of projected possibilities out of the past calls us forward into the future without collapsing the present into the past in a way that would make the past our future. The continuing tension of distance is not underplayed in interpretation as Gadamer is in the end, inclined to do (as we shall see below).

For him it would appear that to speak of horizons rather than horizon arises in the context of an ontological fallenness and is necessary only as that which is on its way to one horizon.

Thus while he accepts the tension within the hermeneutical situation he does not allow it a continued existence within the fusion of horizons which it must have if it is to be truly dialectical. He is led at times due to his negative view of distance to asserting the formation of one horizon. What is required is a more positive evaluation of distance which recognizes that despite the fusion one horizon cannot be reduced to the other – the tensions cannot be removed. One need not accept Nietzche's radical non-communicative pluralism nor Gadamer's occasional tendency to accept the non-hermeneutical position of a single horizon containing all points of view – which runs against the main thrust of his thinking – in order to realise that the fusion of horizons implies a tension between what is one's own and what is alien, between the near and the far; and hence the play of difference is included in the process of convergence. The *identity* which emerges from and in the fusion of horizons is an *identity-in-difference*.

We can learn much from Hegel at this point who, despite this concept of absolute knowledge or a single horizon, presents us with a dialectical thinking which has a lot to teach us along the way. The concept of 'negation' which plays such an important part in his dialectic is based on the proposition that any particular opens towards the universal in that it calls forth the other as part of its definition. We have already said that this is the case within any particular tradition of the Church in that it requires the concept of catholicity if it is to be a credible Christian tradition – for Hegel identity is recognised as it is and could be. An immobile self-contained selfhood is the height of subjective illusion. In his *Phenomonology of Spirit* he gives a penetrating critique of 'sense certainty' which is analogous to the egotistic selfhood which we have rejected as a possibility. This sense certainty 'believes that it can have a perception of the thing in itself – the particular shorn of its essential relationships which are constitutive of the thing as it is. Pure perception of anything breaks down because it fails to recognise that even the internal relationship of a thing to itself is a negative-in-positive relationship. G.R.G. Mure puts it in this way:

> If we recognise a finite thing so changing that it remains recognizably self same after change . . We will admit that it is . . . a positive in negative, a concrete unity determined – that is negated – in and through the diverse phases of its temporal process.[3]

This is exactly what we have been saying about the hermeneutical relationship we have in preserving our particular traditions. "On the other hand . . . if otherness between the elements of one finite thing is their mutual determining of finite things . . . The unique individuality of . . . this thing breaks down as soon as we see that finite things by virtue of the host of common characteristics which they share, and through the network of relations in which they stand, do deeply determine each other's nature."[4] This is what we have been saying is the case between tradition. (Irish traditions?)

123

As Hegel sees it this 'pure perception' mode of reasoning cannot exist for long and passes to the other extreme in which it loses its conception of otherness. The tension between one finite thing or person and another is broken down by making otherness disappear into selfhood – his famous master-slave relationship is a good example. This also fails because just as identity cannot be maintained on the basis of this one thing in the midst of pure and undialectical otherness neither can it be maintained on the basis of a collapse of otherness into selfhood. Selfhood which does not see itself as the whole demands recognition by and of otherness. Self-consciousness is a reflective reality which establishes identity in encounter with and appropriation of what is 'other' or different.

In Hegel's works all of this moves on towards absolute knowledge which is a denial of the finite. Nevertheless, it is, as we have said, the dialectical process itself and not Hegel's intentions which is important for us. What his dialectical description provides us with is the possibility of the explication of the truth of wholeness and not the whole or absolute truth. His mistake was to confuse the two. What he has shown is that in the realm of historicity the dialectic moves by way of negation and affirmation. A would appear to be in opposition to B but this absolute dichotomy breaks down and a fusion or synthesis appears. This synthesis is itself not without tensions – it is an identity – in – difference – and it in turn proves to be inadequate in the new situation and so on. Having rejected Hegel's absolute synthesis, we can say that within an ontology of finitude any fusion is superior only in the sense of relative adequacy to the situation in which it comes about. There is no absolute superiority either behind us or in front of us. Any fusion will inevitably break down because of its internal tensions and relative inadequacy to new and different historical situations. Otherness may assume a new form and so may identity but both will always be unsurpassable reality. Paul Tillich sums up the implications of this for our study very well.

> The ecumenical movement . . is able to heal divisions which have become historically obsolete, to replace confessional fanaticism by interconfessional co-operation . . but neither the ecumenical movement nor any future movement can conquer the ambiguity of unity and division in the Church's historical existence. Even if it were able to produce the United Churches of the world and even if all latent churches were converted to this unity, new divisions would appear. The dynamics of life, the tendency to preserve the holy . . the ambiguities in the sociological existence of the churches, and above all, the prophetic criticism and demand for reformation would bring about new and, in many cases, spiritually justified divisions.[5]

Any glossing over this by attempts to bring about one visible organism as the Church is an abstraction from the real ecumenical task of finding identity-in-difference.

124

## Section Three

*Fusion and Critique*

Gadamer's conception of tradition is in the end monolithic because it does not account for the encounter of traditions and the critique that a genuine encounter between them involves. If he were to take such into consideration he would be forced to consider the possibility of certain facets of tradition being challenged and that challenge being sustained. Only within a positive evaluation of distance is this possible or probable – "to see ourselves as others see us" implies distanciation as a productive force. This is why ecumenics is so vital so that we can view and be viewed within the perspective of belonging distance. We will never attain a true self consciousness or be challenged by fudged issues or blurred distinctions or as *Vatican Two* puts it "Nothing is so foreign to the Spirit of ecumenics as a false conciliatory approach."[6]

But must we go further still? It may well be that a retrieval of and fusion of horizons between the central instances of our traditions will expose our mis-understandings or even our individual traditional distortions but what about those we may share? If ecumenics is not to be involved at least in part in a fusion of illusions, a parallelling of distortions or an allurement of harmful interests, conversation must include a common critique. Consensus is no guarantee of truth. Here we are involved in the kind of debate which exists between Gadamer and Habermas.[7] If Gadamer is concerned with the renewal of and interpretation of tradition and culture, Habermas is concerned to unmask their illusions and distortions. Gadamer will not allow, his rejection of distance cannot allow, the elevation of a critical moment to seriously challenge the authority of tradition. Habermas suggests that it is precisely this authority which must be challenged if we are to be freed – for his real interest is liberation – from its distortions of com-munication; for Gadamer hermeneutics is about understanding and unmasking misunderstanding; for Habermas this displays a traditional innocence and an inno-cent tradition which history does not bear out, for Gadamer it is the authority of the past which predominates, for Habermas it is the "pull of the future". Neither of these men are concerned with ecumenics but they are concerned with hermeneutics. We have seen why Gadamer's conception of tradition, while it is in many ways fundamental, is in the end inadequate to the ecumenical reality and task. When we approach the problem of critique this inadequacy is at its most ob-vious. Can Habermas help us? We are concerned with possible distortions: we are as an eschatological faith concerned with the pull of the future and we recognise the ambiguity of our ecclesial existence and traditions. Without therefore following Habermas in detail we may conclude that what he suggests is missing in Gadamer's hermeneutics is, at least in part, necessary in our ecumenics with regard to our own traditions and Christianity in general. Were not Tetzel's actions a distortion of the faith and of human dignity, was it not based on economic interest? Is not the Reformed Church of South Africa practising a distorted ecclessial life based on racism and racist interests? Is not the entire Christian tradition guilty of a distortion of the Jewish question – a distortion possibly going back even into the New Testament itself? Are we capable of treating women as equals merely on the basis of the authority of the Christian tradition? Does an answer to these questions mean that in finding it we will have had to leave a conversation with our traditions behind and be guided instead by the future? The answer is, yes, if by leaving behind we mean we must not repeat but it is, no, if we mean by leaving behind we consider our traditions as having no further relevance. Our traditions present us with models of liberation – Exodus, Resurrection, etc. – models of how to begin again, models of discipline and the denial of self interest – models of reconciliation. Critique is also a tradition and this is nowhere truer than in the Christian faith. Where are we to find the resources to envisage our future if not in encounter – in conversation – with our past? While the past must not take the future prisoner neither can it breach all the bounds. It is a radical belonging which promises freedom. Again as Ricoeur so aptly suggests "perhaps there would be no more interest in emancipation, no more anticipation of freedom, if the Exodus and the Resurrection were effaced from the memory of mankind".[8] Nevertheless we must address the future and sustained address demands that we also address the possible distortions in our past. Emancipation cannot simply be based on the past anymore than can consensus. One cannot speak with Gadamer of a common accord which carries understanding without assuming a convergence of traditions which does not exist, without hypostatising a past which is also the place of false consciousness, without ontologising a language which has always only been a distorted 'communication competence'.[9] This is indeed an overstatement of the case and was not written regarding ecumenics – but it could have been.

*Conclusion*

To sum up, we have suggested that we must recognise identity as a dialectical rather than a static or conflictual reality and that its preservation demands a mutual learning process between 'our' and 'other' traditions. For the most part we have not directly addressed the political questions but in that there is no absolute dichotomy between theological or political questions – particularly in Ireland – such questions and the direction of our thinking upon them is fairly obvious.

One of the problems, however, in any political analogies is that one section of the Irish people has an inadequately developed sense of 'belonging', i.e. the 'Protestant people of Ulster' and it is only if this belonging can be fostered and nurtured that any genuine fusion can take place.

Perhaps only the 'pull of the future' can make this possible. A pull in which all our traditions must be transformed into living, liberating praxis. Here again it is as we accept the distance between ourselves and the myths, symbols and events of our past traditions that such a liberated belonging is possible.

## NOTES

1. *Truth and Method*, Sheed and Ward, London 1976, pp. 241-5.
2. Paul Ricoeur; *Hermeneutics and the Human Sciences*. Ed. and translated by John B. Thompson, Cambridge, Cambridge University Press, 1981, p.93.
3. *The Philosophy of Hegel*, Oxford, 1965, p.14.
4. *Ibid.*
5. *Systematic Theology*, Vol. 3. London, S.C.M. 1963, p.169.
6. *The Documents of Vatican Two*, Ed. by Walter M. Abbott, S.J., London, Geoffrey Chapman, 1967, p.354.
7. For two recent surveys of this debate see, Paul Ricoeur, *Hermeneutics and the Human Sciences*, Ch.2, pp. 63-100 and also *Irish Philosophical Journal*, Vol.2, No.1, Spring 1985. *Religion and Ideology: Paul Ricoeur's Hermeneutic Conflict* (pp. 37-52) by Richard Kearney.
8. *Ibid*, pp. 99-100.
9. *Ibid*, p.87.

# The Reconciliation of Memories

*Mark Santer*

Why is the category of 'memory' so important? Memory is important because of the crucial role it plays in relation to our sense of identity. A person with amnesia has lost his identity, except what can be reconstructed from other peoples' researches and memories. It is through our memories, through our recollection of the past, and through what others have told us about the past, that we identify ourself as who we are.

Most of our memories are in some way social. We identify ourselves in relation to other people – our parents, our brothers and sisters, our friends and our enemies. We also identify ourselves as members of groups – this group over against that group, this family over against that, this church over against that. And so our identity is marked not only by what we ourselves, as individuals, can remember, but by the corporate memories of the group, and by what others have told us about the past we share if we belong to that group. To give a simple example, there are things about my early childhood which I can certainly remember for myself; but there are others of which I am not sure whether I really remember them myself or whether I *think* I remember them because I've been told about them.

Memory, whether individual or corporate, is always selective. We cannot remember everything. We remember the things we need to or want to remember, or things which have affected us so deeply that we cannot help remembering them. We remember things and people and events by telling stories about them. So there's not only selection, there's also interpretation, and interpretation in the selection. Some things, important to others, we simply will not notice or recall. Our choice is largely unreflective.

So it is striking how often it is that two people, present at the same event, will give two different accounts of it. This is especially obvious when there has been a quarrel or some other break of communication. We fall out with someone – and cannot even agree what it is we are arguing about. Commonly, if an injury is thought to have been done, it will be remembered and nursed by the party that thinks itself injured, while the party complained of may not even have noticed that hurt has been done. This is true of a family row; it is also true of communal grievances. So Irishmen have a story about what Oliver Cromwell did at Drogheda; it's important to their identity. Englishmen have no story about it at all; either it's not important at all or else it's been important to forget it. At all events, part of the Irish grievance is precisely the lack of English awareness.

We maintain our communal identity not only by stories, but also by festivals and rituals, and by stories embedded in ritual. That, after all, is what we do whenever we celebrate the Eucharist. By remembering Christ's death, resurrection and coming again we remind ourselves of our identity as Christians. This remembrance is powerfully focussed in the eating of bread and the sharing of a cup of wine in remembrance of his sacrificial death.

Similarly, the traditional Christian ceremonies of Holy Week and Easter are a powerful means whereby Christians identify themselves through their ritual remembrance of Christ's entry into Jerusalem, his last supper, his betrayal, his death and resurrection. This is wonderful for Christians. But the potential ambiguity of all such rituals of group identity comes out, when we remember what Holy Week was often like for the Jews of Eastern Europe. Then we see what happens when an in-group of the accepted requires an out-group of the rejected.

And so we naturally think of the rituals by which groups of divided Christians have marked themselves off from each other, and have kept the grievances alive which sustain their own identity over against their rivals. Thus Fox's *Book of Martyrs* used to be Sunday reading for English Protestants. Guy Fawkes Day was, and in some places still is, an annual celebration of Anti-Popery. The Roman Catholics in England have fervently treasured the memories of their martyrs, put to death by a State whole religious face was the Church of England. In this company I hardly need mention the Green and Orange martyrs of Ireland.

We all need our stories and our rituals. As I said at the beginning, without our memories we have no identity. But our memories are as subject to the effects of sin as the rest of our human condition. We abuse this gift of memory when we employ it for keeping ourselves in the right and others in the wrong, for keeping grievances alive and for perpetuating stereotypes which justify us in treating other groups in demeaning, or oppressive ways. Thus: women are irrational; Irish are stupid; criminals are animals; the unemployed are idle; you can never trust the Russians.

All of these points are important in thinking about communical conflicts of any kind. They have obvious relevance to conflicts between peoples and nations. But my particular experience is in trying to deal with religious conflict – conflict between groups which have rival accounts, rival stories, of why it is that they are divided. All conflicts produce histories – as we can see from the blossoming of history writing in the fourth and fifth centuries (celebrating the conflicts with paganism and between Orthodoxy and Arianism) and in the wake of the Reformation. The Protestant story had to be met by the Catholic story, and vice versa. Let us notice a few things of which we must be aware in trying to move out of conflict towards reconciliation – points of which I myself have become aware through ecumenical work.

(i) Although doctrinal differences are of great importance, since our apprehension of the truth of the Gospel is at stake, it is mistaken to think that our differences are simply matters of doctrine, or that it is theologians alone who keep Christians apart. The ecumenical task is not to reconcile theologies, but to reconcile the people and communities who use those theologies to identify themselves as distinct from each other. Theological differences become intractable when they become a function of one group's identity over against another, or have become the flags marking an institutional frontier. Once they have become badges of identity, such issues are kept alive by the need to tell a story which justifies the maintenance of the status quo of separation in face of the gospel demand for reconciliation. The attraction of doctrinal issues is that they appear to allow us to remain divided with a good conscience.

Thus Protestants keep justification by faith alive as an issue, precisely because their self-identity depends on a story which characterises Roman Catholics as people who do not believe in it. Similarly, English and Irish Roman Catholics, who for centuries suffered persecution and disadvantage at the hands of a state which had identified "Transubstantiation" as the litmus-paper of subversion, are reluctant to believe that there is nothing to argue about after all. It's not simply a matter of theology; it's a question of group identity.

(ii) Differences which we can live with within one communion become intolerable once there has been a breakdown of trust and once this breakdown has become institutionalised, it becomes extremely difficult to persuade people that they do not justify division. The doctrine of justification by faith is a good example. In fact, disputes on justification, predestination, grace and good works raged in the pre-reformation church and among both Protestants and Catholics after the Reformation. The issues are complex, and by no means clear-cut. There is no doubt that there are differences of emphasis which one can broadly identify as Protestant and Catholic. yet, as soon as one tries to show that, on basic points, we share a common faith, and that differences of emphasis should not be church-dividing, we are charged with papering-over cracks, or of pretending that the historical disputes were simply a matter of verbal misunderstanding.

(iii) Once we are divided, we tend in our minds to pickle our opponents in the past. So a modern Protestant will imagine that, in dealing with the Roman Catholic Church, he must still be dealing with the abuse which outraged Luther. He will feel disorientated and upset if he is told that indulgences are hardly the issue today which they were 450 years ago. If a Roman Catholic tells him this, he will think that he's not a real Roman Catholic; and if I tell him, he will think that I have been deceived, either by Roman Catholic guile or by my own gullibility.

If we do not know a community at first hand, we tend to pin it down to its published documents, while making allowances for development and interpretation in dealing with our own. Thus Protestants who are suspicious of Roman Catholics will insist on reading ARCIC in the light of Trent as they themselves have traditionally understood it. They are reluctant to allow modern

Roman Catholics to speak for themselves.

(iv) As I have already said, we often disagree as to what the argument is about. What seems to one party the crucial issue may not be of interest to the other at all. Justification is a good example. For the Protestant, that is what the Reformation was about; and if the Roman Catholic has not even heard of the doctrine – and far less regards it a matter for dispute – that, in Protestant eyes is still further evidence of Roman Catholic error on the point.

Furthermore, even when we agree that there is an issue to be resolved – and that is the case if only one party thinks that there is an issue at stake – then we often disagree on how to approach that issue. Purgatory and indulgences are a good example. They are part of the Roman Catholic lumber, and Protestants keep reviving them – not because they are important now, but because they *were* important 450 years ago and so are part of the story of why we are Protestants. But then the question arises: how do we deal with them? For Protestants, they belong in the context of justification; for Catholics, their proper context is the doctrine of the Church.

(v) No theological agreement exists *in vacua*. It has to be received by the communities which are represented by the theologians. If the agreements are not received and accepted when they are made, the work will have to be done again. Thus, for instance, the degree of theological reconciliation achieved in the Anglican-Methodist conversations of the 1960's cannot be regarded as still on the table. The communities which came so close have moved on. In fact, church history is littered with agreements which have come to nothing because communities have failed to receive them – for instance, in the fifth century, the Christological agreement between the schools of Alexandria and Antioch fell apart; in the fifteenth, the agreements of the Council of Florence were repudiated by the Orthodox people of Constantinople; in the sixteenth, the agreement of Ratisbon on justification was accepted neither in Rome nor in Wittenberg; and so on. It is not sufficient for the theologians to learn to trust and understand one another.

So what must we do? Three points –

(i) *Friendship* and *trust,* at all levels, are indispensable. We must learn to talk to and listen *to* each other, and not just talk *about* each other. As long as we just read about other Christians, we shall persist in our fantasies – just as we persist in our fantasies about Eastern Europe if we never visit it and talk to people who live there.

Linked with friendship and trust is the matter of *will* and *desire*. If we do not desire reconciliation, we shall never have it, and it will be a comparatively easy matter to think of reasons of high principle for not being reconciled yet. We shall never get anywhere if we always demand change from the others, and never face up to the fact that repentance and change is also required of us.

Of course there will always be differences between Christians – as there are between husband and wife. But if we are committed to each other, we can face our differences as a shared and common problem, rather than use them as a reason for continuing to mistrust one another.

(ii) Part of our growth in trust is that we should listen to each other's stories. Thus, or instance, English Anglicans need to learn about the Catholic martyrs. We need to learn to share each other's celebrations, and to purge our own of those elements which depend on the denigration or misperception of our rivals. It is very good that when Pope Paul VI canonized the Forty English Martyrs, he did it in a way which included rather than excluded Anglicans. Again, in announcing the Pope's intention to beatify more martyrs on All Saints Day this year, both Cardinal Hume and Archbishop Runcie took care to see them as witnesses to the One Christ, in whose service both Protestants and Catholics have borne witness even to death.

Sharing each other's stories involves sharing each other's festivals and rituals. Here the liturgical movement and the eucharistic revival are helping Christian people to recognize that what is being celebrated is a common faith. The increase in the practice of inter-communion, whatever the authorities may say, is a datum of theological significance.

(iii)  Finally – does it need saying – there was and is no reconciliation without the Cross. Every time we celebrate the Eucharist, we recall or remember the price of our reconciliation. We cannot recall the cross without recalling the sins which put the Lord on the cross – the sins by which we still crucify ourselves and each other. It is as we acknowledge our past – by bringing into conscious memory those things whose consciousness we have repressed – that the cross becomes the means of our healing. We have to forgive and let ourselves be forgiven.

Thereby we are united with Christ in his work of reconciliation. As ministers of reconciliation, we are not simply beneficiaries of the cross. We are called to share in Christ's work of redemption. That means, as you know very well, receiving and bearing the fear and suspicions and even hatred of those who cannot bear to think of reconciliation. In asking people to look at their memories, we are threatening their identity. So no wonder they fight back. It's no good despising them. We need the gifts of patience and love. This is a real sharing of the cross. In working for reconciliation between Christians we are engaged in a fight with truly demonic powers, and we cannot expect to remain unscathed. But this is the point at which we show that we have a gospel, not just for the individual, but for the world. Those who belong to Christ are to live together in one communion as a sign that that is what human beings are made for. That is why theologians talk about *koinonia*: we are created, not to live apart, telling bad stories about one another, but to share a common life, whose image is both the simple table of the last supper, and the city of God whose gates are open to all the nations.

# Contributors

Maurice Bond        is pursuing doctoral studies at Trinity College, Dublin, and is presently the Minister of the Presbyterian Church in Ballynahinch, Northern Ireland.

Gabriel Daly        an Augustinian priest, is Lecturer in Theology at Trinity College, Dublin, and the Irish School of Ecumenics. His published works include *Transcendence and Immanence* (1980) and *Asking the Father* (1982).

Séamus Deane        is Professor of Modern English and American Literature at University College, Dublin. A poet and a literary critic, his publications include *History Lessons* (1983) and *A Short History of Irish Literature* (1986).

Alan Falconer        a Church of Scotland Minister, teaches Theology at the Irish School of Ecumenics. His publications include (ed) *Understanding Human Rights* (1980) and *A Man Alone* (1987).

Joe Harris        taught Education at the University of Ulster, Coleraine, and has pioneered programmes on the theme of reconciling memories, above all in encouraging young people to understand the religious traditions in Ireland.

Richard Kearney        teaches Philosophy at University College, Dublin. A member of the Field Day Group and editor of *The Crane Bag*, his most recent publications include *Transitions* (1987).

Joseph Liechty        an American Mennonite, is undertaking postgraduate research at St. Patrick's College, Maynooth.

Margaret MacCurtain    teaches History at University College, Dublin, and is Superior of her Dominican community. A frequent author of articles on historical and women's movement themes, she is an editor of the Gill and Macmillan History of Ireland series.

Mark Santer        is the Bishop of Birmingham and the Anglican co-Chairman of the Anglican-Roman Catholic International Commission. His published works include (ed) *Their Lord and Ours* (1982).

Frank Wright       teaches Political Science at Queen's University, Belfast. He is a member of the Corrymeela Community and has published *Northern Ireland: A comparative analysis* (1987).

# Index

Act of Union, 76
Acton, Lord, 34
Alexandra, School of, 131
Anglican-Methodist conversations, 131
Anglo-Irish tradition, iv, 3, 54, 68, 75
Antioch, School of, 131
ARCIC, 130
Arendt, Hannah, 85
Aristotle, 114
Arnold, Matthew, 25
Ashe, Thomas, 10
Asquith, Lord, 73
Atonement, 37, 90ff, 100
Auden, W.H., 84
Auschwitz, 107 ff.,
Badeni decrees, 73
Ball, Hugo, 39
Ballymascanlon, 31
Barth, Karl 113
Barthes, Roland, 12
Bateson, Gregory, 39
Beckett, John, 3, 21, 31
Behan, Brendan, 104
BEM, 6
Benjamin, Walter, 9
Berlin, Isaiah, 106
Bias, in history, 33ff.
Black & Tans, 32
Bond, Maurice, 116ff
Bonhoeffer, Dietrich, 4
Bowen, Desmond, 52
Boyd, Rev.Dr.R.H.S., i
British Utilitarians, 25
Brunner, Emil, 86
Bultmann, Rudolph, 13
Burckhardt, Jacob, 87
Calvin, John, 93
Castoriadis, 38

Catholic Defenders, 76
Celtic art, 3
Chalcedon, Council of, 112
Christian Unity, 73, 116ff
Civil Rights Movement 74
Clarke, Austin, 1, 20 25
Clanricarde, Earl of, 59
Connolly, James, 53 ff.
Cruise O'Brien, Conor, 53
Constantinople, Orthodox Church, 131
Corish, Rev. Patrick, 4
Crane Bag, The, 3, 8
Crawford, Sharman, 82
Crichton Smith, Iain, 4,5
Cromwell, Oliver, 128
Culture – Irish, 19ff, 25ff, 31,37ff.
Curry, John, 56
Czechoslovakia, 1
Dallmayr, 47
Daly, Rev.Gabriel, 99
Dante, 26
Davis, Charles, 114
Davis, Thomas, 25
Deane, Séamus, 11, 25ff, 36
Descartes, 116
de Valera, President Eamon, 31
Devlin, Denis, 25
Dillistone, F.W., 100
Drummond, Thomas, 76
Dublin University Magazine, 25
Dutch-North Ireland Committee, i
Duffy, Charles Gavan, 82
Earls, The, 2
Ecclesiastical Titles Bill, 82
Eliade, Mircea, 14, 27
Eliot, T.S., 84
Ephesians, 90
Fascism, 17

135